19 COVID LESSONS
the Church Cannot Ignore

Why "Back to Normal" Is Not an Option

NATANAEL COSTEA

Published by Evangelista Media & Consulting
www.evangelistamedia.com
publisher@evangelistamedia.com

ISBN: 978-88-6880-124-3
Ebook ISBN: 978-88-6880-109-0

For Worldwide Distribution
1 2 3 4 5 6 / 23 22 21 20

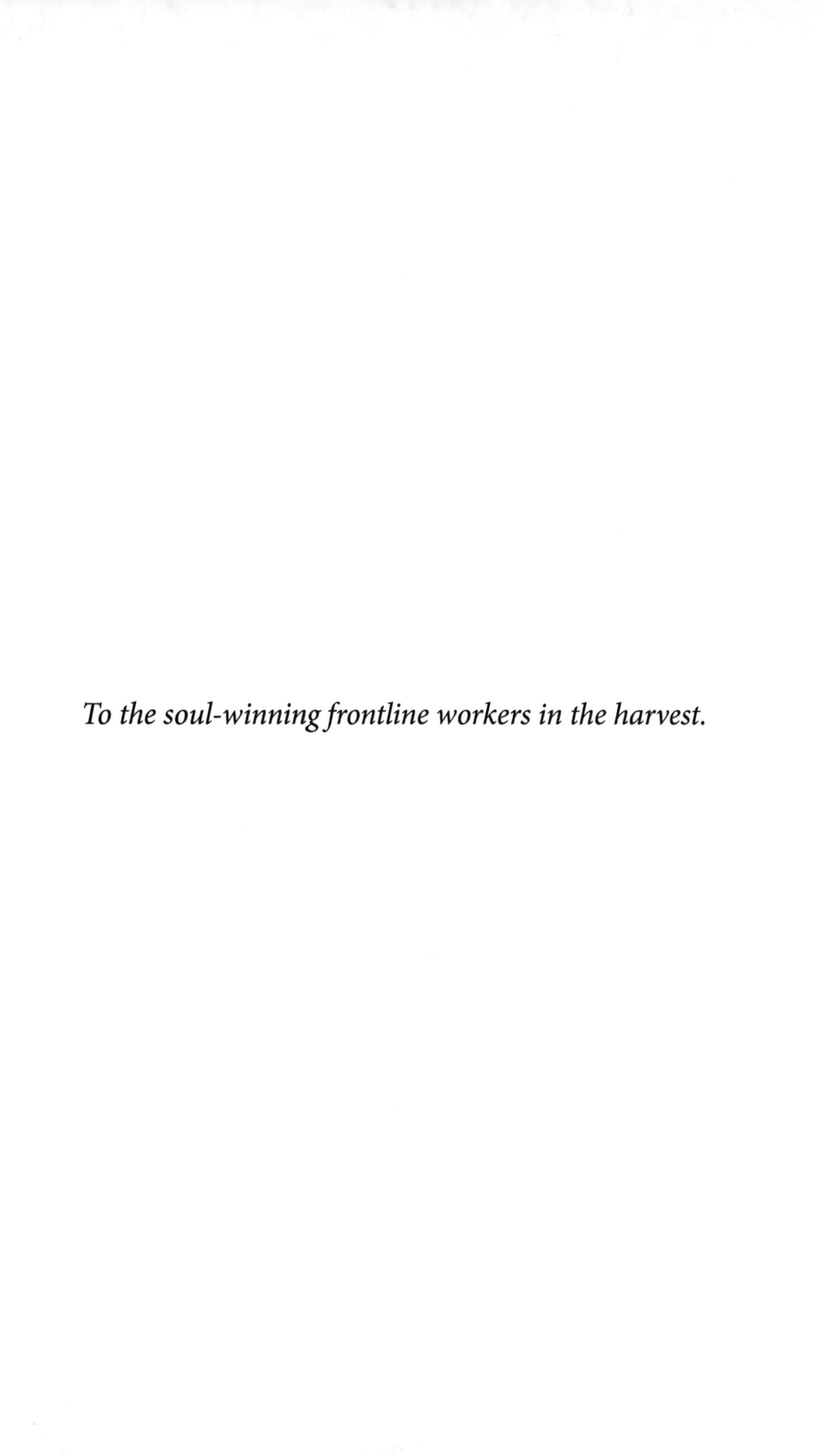

To the soul-winning frontline workers in the harvest.

ENDORSEMENTS

This book is a genuine collection of the problems besetting contemporary mainstream Western Christianity, accompanied by a creative call to return to a genuine Christ-centered form of life and ministry. Truthfulness and fruitfulness are its marks. This is a sure sign of its true prophetic teaching, the very antithesis of popularity. If you are looking for significant disruption out of a worldly Church and a deeper discipleship walk with the Lord, read it as an act of indispensable submission on the way of the cross.

Rev. Dr. John Yates, Chairman
Evangelical Alliance Australia

In this current season that the nations of the earth find themselves, there is a required response that must come from the Church of Jesus Christ as the ambassadors of the kingdom of God on earth. It has been said that testing times are the moments that champions are revealed. In this book, Dr. Natanael Costea outlines a roadmap of sorts with regard to the questions that leaders from the body of Christ need to be asking and answering dynamically through their church and ministry expressions.

Natanael is a dynamic leader, thinker, builder, and practitioner of kingdom realities and brings to bear much biblical wisdom and insights that will empower church leaders to make clear and powerful decisions as they lead their churches and enterprises through this crisis. I highly recommend not only this book but also Natanael as an apostolic minister to the body of Christ.

David Balestri, National Convenor
Australian Coalition of Apostolic Leaders

▪◇▪▪◇▪

In the midst of restriction and disruption flowing from the COVID-19, the Church and particularly church leaders have been confronted with the need to quickly adapt to the changing landscape. Dr. Natanael Costea has provided here a challenging and thought-provoking resource to assist Church leaders to take hold of God's *opportune* time for RESET. By raising penetrating questions that need prayerful and careful exploration he provides a way to reevaluate how we think about church and do ministry going forward. Be prepared to be challenged and to push deeper!

Len Rossow, Facilitator
Gold Coast House of Prayer
Gold Coast, Queensland, Australia

▪◇▪▪◇▪

Dr. Natanael Costea has written a very timely and much needed book. He writes not only as a strong teacher with clear biblical lessons, he also writes as an experienced coach, providing provoking questions at the end of each chapter, so we are challenged to make changes. And change is needed in these days. Natanael is a tender prophetic voice challenging the Church, you and I, to listen closely to the Lord and to reset, recalibrate, and be part of a much needed reformation in our day.

Wendy Yapp, Facilitator
Perth Together, Australia

As a missionary in Indonesia and the Middle East, I helped establish a church of 20,000 and assisted in planting over 2,000 churches through my students. I faced many challenges and learned that only God has the answers to overcome. Now, Dr. Natanael Costea has issued a timely challenge in the face of a global COVID-19 pandemic. Do we really understand what it is to be a Christian in these times? Do we understand what it means to acknowledge the lordship of Jesus? Do we comprehend the depths of revelation, joy, friendship and love of learning to walk as Christ's Church and to live in true fellowship and discipleship? The COVID-19 global pandemic has created an opportunity for Christians to draw near to Christ, return to a biblical vision of what is in the heart of God, and to be the people in this generation that the Lord wants us to be.

Dr. Costea's book, *19 Covid Lessons the Church Cannot Ignore* provides clarity, faith, and uncomfortable questions which must be answered; but in this time of crisis, we should open our minds and hearts and dare to implement the biblical principles presented to us. The time has never been riper for a return to what Jesus taught us and to see the eternal purpose of God begin to become a reality in our generation. This book is filled with great Bible studies and principles that challenge us not to return to the old normal but to face the reality of our generation and to rise up and respond in humble repentance, biblical faith, and a love and commitment to the pathway given to us by Christ.

One challenge that comes across may be uncomfortable: Do we want to get "our" church up and running again, or do we want to be the Church that Jesus wants for this generation? Are we praying, "My will be done?" or "Thy will be done?"

19 Covid Lessons the Church Cannot Ignore is a must-read book. It contains many revolutionary concepts, biblical truths that we cannot ignore if we want to be the kind of Christians Jesus wants us to be.

Dr. Jeff Hammond
Abbahouse Ministries
Kialla, Victoria, Australia

Dr. Natanael Costea is one of a new breed of Christian leaders who are being raised up by God to prepare the body of Christ for a new wave of the Holy Spirit. He knows who he is in Christ and has the courage to stand up and be counted as a true disciple of Jesus. This book encapsulates the very heart of God and is a wakeup call to the New Testament Church to consider in order to survive these and future dark times. I would encourage people to take the challenges this book makes and to have a major paradigm shift in their thinking as to who we really are in Christ.

Ps. Malcolm Innes, President
Dayspring Ministries, Australia
Apostolic Churches Alliance Board

In the middle of this pandemic engulfing everyone with fear, the question should not be how to return to the old normal life. It should be, as Dr. Natanael Costea writes, what is the Lord teaching us for the season ahead. Read it with your ears tuned in so you hear what the Lord is saying to you, and move in that direction.

Vali Paul, Senior Pastor
Filadelfia Church
Baia Mare, Romania

Dr. Natanael Costea has done a commendable study of each critically important topic presented, and provides thoughts to help absorb, understand, and respond appropriately. It will be particularly helpful to church leaders and members who are seeking to respond and remain relevant, missional, and transformational following the massive changes brought upon our world by the COVID-19 crisis. One of my own observations is that as responsible leaders in the Church of our Lord Jesus Christ we must be constantly seeking objective truth.

This truth needs to be gleaned from official as well as trusted unofficial and more importantly heavenly sources, and be guided by the wisdom of God to discern what to do and say in public and in private in order to uphold and advance the kingdom of God with integrity, in all domains of our society. Please enjoy this worthy work.

David Apelt, Apostle and Senior Pastor
Hillview Community Church and Apostolic Centre
Southern Cross Association of Churches
Australian Coalition of Apostolic Leaders

The alarm bell has been ringing in 2020. The risk to health and many deaths, serious economic impact and travel restrictions have disrupted normal life and limited church attendance. We can quickly recognize worldwide problems, but what about seeing the causes and identifying solutions. Could it be God has a message for us or an unseen challenge to alert the Church? Yes, a challenge. Consider the many wake-up calls the Church received over the last 100 years. God has attempted to gain our attention frequently, but with so few responses. What can we do? Is the answer in the following 19 chapters?

This book will make you think and act hopefully to respond to God's latest wake-up call to a *sleeping giant* Church. Wake up, Church! Awaken and influence the world by displaying power and authority, and equipping and mobilizing Jesus' disciples. Raise churchgoers from their *spectator* seats to become participants *seeking and saving* the lost and encourage disciples in obedience as they GO responding to Jesus' command.

Ps. Jeff Hocking, Board
Apostolic Churches Alliance

This book is a one-of-a-kind resource that you must have in your personal library and a treasure to read. It is a true revelation of our current crisis and self-examination of every leader and pastor. Not only does it speak about the contemporary Church but it is a measuring scale, a plumb line, a temperature gauge of our motives and attitudes. This is a pastor's crisis management manual.

Dr. Costea takes a pastor on a journey from where the roots of the Church were to where it is, and it is heading. I would call it an extraordinary book, a must read for every pastor. As I was reading, I found it to be so true and so apt to our times and seasons. It is doctrinally sound, Bible based, and prayerfully written. You will not be able to put the book down once you get started. This book gives you an outlook of your church, your life, and your ministry.

Dr. Andrew Prakasam, President
Share in Asia
A242 Outlook Church Founding Pastor

◆■◆

Based on sound scriptural narratives and divine revelation, Dr. Natanael Costea challenges the church not only to navigate a new normal through the COVID-19 season but to return to our first love of Jesus, authentic relationships, and hail Jesus as the Head of the Church. He also reassures us and encourages us that God has a plan for the Church through this time of spiritual warfare and will use it to bring His glory and see more souls saved. With practical questions for application, you will be both challenged and refreshed to go bigger and bolder out of this season.

Dr. Reg Morais, Founder
Anoint the World Ministries
Living Faith Community Church Senior Pastor

I have known Pastor Natanael Costea for sixteen years as someone who loves God very much and has become a true brother and friend. He came to the hinterland of West Kalimantan, Indonesia, to set up schools where the first generation of indigenous Dayak children are educated and to build churches in towns and villages with no places of worship. I say this to give you a glimpse of how the Lord has seasoned and matured him in the trenches of first line tribal mission ministry.

The current pandemic has proven a great equalizer in the world as wealth and society position give no safety to anyone. Everyone is afraid. The only solution, as this book highlights, is for everyone to return to God and reestablish the family altar and allow God to reform ministry in the Church. The book reminds us of the work of the Holy Spirit to change us, to comfort us, to teach us, and to strengthen us. Everyone who will read this book will be encouraged in an extraordinary way to rise up to the current challenge and also the opportunity at hand.

Pdt. Pustikawati Djunaidi, Pastor
Gereja Bethel Indonesia, Gloria Tikalong, West Kalimantan

Knowing Dr. Natanael Costea for more than 40 years and seeing the call of God so clearly on his life from an early age, I can fully agree with Dr. Bob Chapman, his spiritual father and professor, that Natanael was his best student. Natanael has always been a very inspiring and devoted leader who gave himself to the Lord's service from a young age.

This timely book is like an alarm clock in the middle of the night calling us to wake up and turn on the light. It provokes us to reevaluate our ways, our motives and even our methods. We cannot go back to our old ways. As the world around us is rapidly changing, God is also drastically changing the landscape of the Church. Things cannot stay the same. This book will help you transition in the new era that God is bringing, so go for it.

Cornel Bistrian, Director
Christ for Romania

It took a worldwide pandemic for someone with an investigative and apostolic mindset to write a book to challenge, stir, and make all of us think again. The future is creeping up on us quicker than what we think.

Most do not like their boat being rocked; but in this well-written book, Natanael Costea talks about rebuilding, restoring, reforming, reestablishing, realigning, and rising to a new kind of church that's on the horizon of God's heart but not yet in reality. This book is a storehouse of twists and turns to keep you on the edge. Great!

Rev. Russell Sage
Sage International Ministries
Perth, Western Australia

DEDICATION

Ministry leaders who have uncompromisingly laid down their lives for their King and Master, Jesus Christ: Every day you earnestly labor in the harvest field! My heart goes to you as you serve the invisible God through the visible humble service to every human soul on your journey. There is no nobler calling.

Frontline workers who risk their lives to save others: You demonstrate a godly concern and care for God's creation. Thank you for your fearless commitment to preserving life.

My late spiritual father, Dr. Bob Chapman [1947–2020]: You loved me as your son and passed me your ministry mantle. I carry it with utmost responsibility. This book is full of the legacy you built in me.

Menora church family: You are the heartbeat of my ministry. Thank you for granting me the privilege to lead you.

My family: We are one. Raluca, my gorgeous wife, you hold me up and keep me going with your undeterred love and commitment to our family journey. I love you. Evangeline, Isaac, and Menora, you are modeling my heart after God's. I bless you with these spiritual insights for this life and beyond.

And to my King: You are the Truth, the Way, and the Life! I honor and glorify You!

CONTENTS

INTRODUCTION

Welcome to April 2020. Unannounced, unexpected and highly unwanted, the coronavirus has crippled the world into a lockdown to an unprecedented scale.

Named COVID-19, which stands for COrona VIrus Disease of 2019, this "pandemic" presumably started in China toward the end of 2019 and rapidly spread throughout the world bringing it to a stall by mid-March and early April 2020. It is a respiratory illness caused by a new virus that can spread from person to person by being in close contact.

Throughout the world we are now in our homes in isolation to prevent the spread. This has been the world's largest social isolation and the church has been disrupted in an unparalleled way. This lockdown means the church cannot meet in their buildings, nor as groups, except as households. It was a shockwave that unsettled both leaders and church members, characterized by an evident resistance in closing the church doors. But this had to be done.

This book is written in the middle of the pandemic that has reported more than 23 million cases, more than 800,000 deaths, and over 15 million recoveries worldwide, so far. The situation may change by the time this book is released, so I will provide an update in the last chapter.

It is 5 a.m. on April 21, 2020, as I start typing this book. I wrestled with the thought for over three weeks—and in the end I felt compelled to write it.

The Lord has a message for us in this uncharted time that is worth sharing. I have been asking myself and God many questions probably like you have, questions that do not necessarily demand an answer, but they do prompt us to inquire:

- What if this is happening *for* us and not *to* us? Is this a pandemic or just a situation?

- Is this from God or not?

- Why is it so difficult to understand what's going on?

- Why is He allowing it?

- What if He's trying to tell us something through this?

- What if He's asking for our attention?

- What if He is using it *for* something, something we may not yet fully understand and comprehend?

When Joseph finally revealed himself to his brothers in Egypt, he had a remarkable *conclusion* to all the unfairness he experienced at the hand of his brothers and at the accusations of Potiphar's wife that landed him in prison for several years. His ending perspective is notable.

> *As for you, you meant evil against me, but God meant it for good, to bring it about that many people should be kept alive, as they are today* (Genesis 50:20).

Joseph saw God in *everything* that was happening to him, no matter how unjust and evil it was. He knew that God had *a plan*, and He was *in control* of everything, *turning it* all around for His purposes. He did, and his nation was kept alive because of it.

This is a *healthy perspective* for us to have as we come to grips with the coronavirus pandemic. The devil wants to steal, kill, and destroy but Jesus, the Good Shepherd brings *abundant life* (John 10:10).

Knowing this, I believe we have a choice: to merely *survive* or to *thrive,* to give in to this pandemic hype by succumbing to *fear* or to rise above it in *faith,* to let it drag us *down* or to allow God to use it for *good.*

The pause button has been placed on church as usual. The world currently speaks of the "new normal." The church had to adapt to new ways, and it had to do it quickly. It does not feel normal because in our conditioning, it isn't. But what if this stir up is for our good?

I believe we will soon have the choice to press play again to church as usual, or better yet, to press reset now. Who dares to press reset? Who feels challenged to look at our ways? Who embraces God's call to consider carefully what we are doing at the personal level and also what the church is doing?

In Lamentations 3:40 there's an invitation to "examine our ways, and return to the LORD!" In a similar way, in Haggai 1 God challenged the people to rebuild the temple. What if in this time He is asking us *to take a real look* at the way we're doing things, especially church. The many questions God was asking the people demanded a thorough consideration. His house was in ruin even though everyone was thriving.

How are we, as the church, traveling at the moment? How healthy is the church currently? Does it need a reset, a rebuild, and a fresh consideration? What if God is inviting us in this time to pause and ask ourselves some deep questions about the way we do church? What if this is *an opportunity* to take stock, to meditate, to jot down and reframe, to go back to His blueprint and rebuild? What if there are lessons from the coronavirus that we can learn, or better yet, we *cannot ignore?*

The world is changing quickly. Governments have had to make rushed decisions. The economy is in uncharted territory and businesses are forced to make radical resolutions. There are major changes happening in all spheres of society at a fast pace. There are massive opportunities at hand in every domain. How will the church respond to this shake? Will it see it as an opportunity to thrive or will it wait for it to be over so it can return to normal?

We *cannot* return to normal! I pray that we *will not!* I pray that we become resolute with immediate effect *to pursue* the new wineskin, the refreshed way of being God's church.

Never before have we had this opportunity. Never before could we return to basics. Never before were we able to pause and consider in a meaningful way what church is all about.

Let's not miss this chance! Let's *not* return to normal! Let's not slide back into the comfortable and predictable! Let's *embrace* this season as a season of *reset, restoration* and *realignment,* which leads us into *renewal* and into *transformation.* And it might just lead us into *reformation.*

Please know that I am a pastor and I write to you as a leader who labors responsibly in God's field. I say this for you to have the confidence that I care deeply as I challenge you in this book. I challenge you because I care. I care for you and I honor you as you serve tirelessly and desire to align more and more with God's will!

Take these lessons to heart. Spend some time with them. Allow the Holy Spirit to guide you into how you can apply them. Seize the current opportunity. Come up higher!

Let each lesson bring at least *one shift* in your personal life and in your church life. Ask yourself what is the one alignment or recalibration the Lord is bringing through each lesson in your personal and church life.

When Jesus met the rich young ruler (see Mark 10:17-22), He asked the ruler to make only *one shift* in his life. Looking at the story we can see this young man having many faults. In our eyes he lacked many things. But Jesus did not look at him the way we do. Jesus looked for what he was missing, not what was wrong with him. He looked for what was lacking, not what was bad in him.

And Jesus, looking at him, loved him, and said to him, "You lack one thing" (Mark 10:21). To Jesus there was only *one thing* he lacked. Why only one? Because Jesus knew that we can only change one thing at a time. But on this shift hung everything else. It was the *one change* that would change *everything* else.

As you embark on this journey of discovering the 19 lessons the church cannot ignore from the coronavirus, may I please ask you to pause and reflect on *one personal* and *one church* shift you will take on from each lesson?

And as you do that, let it be a shift that will be a game changer for your personal life and ministry life, a shift that puts everything else in *alignment*, a transforming shift to *maturity* and *completion* that leaves you without lacking anything (James 1:4).

The Author

CHAPTER 1

RISE TO THE CHALLENGE

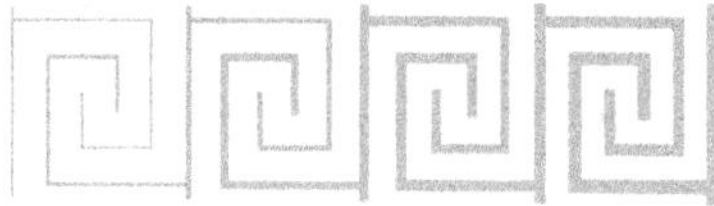

*I know how to be brought low, and I know how to abound.
In any and every circumstance, I have learned the secret of
facing plenty and hunger, abundance and need.*

—Philippians 4:12

The Challenges

→ *The coronavirus lockdown has affected everyone, everywhere.*

→ *Many are living in denial and are looking for other causes.*

→ *The church needs to come to grip with the situation.*

→ *The church needs to lead its people through this period.*

As the news of the coronavirus hit the airwaves, it produced a whirlwind that unsettled the whole world. No one was ready for this challenge, not even the church. The coronavirus pandemic, characterized by a world lockdown, brought uncertainty, fear, and desperation. And the church wasn't spared.

For my wife and I, the greatest challenge was to accept that this was happening and to rise above it. It was hard to believe and we wanted to deny it. It took us a few days to come to terms with this reality. We were taken through a rollercoaster of emotions reading news articles and watching some videos through the social media. It wasn't good news. There was no healthy outlook.

To make matters worse, conspiracy theories began to spring out from a multitude of sources, including church leaders. The views began to be rather skewed but in some way, because of the new sudden uncertainty, quite credible.

After a few days of being drawn into this downward spiral, I rebelled. You see, I am usually a person who does not conform. I grew up in communist Romania in a Judeo-Christian family until the age of 15 when we migrated to Australia. We were regimented to conform, and that developed a deep desire not to.

My rebellion was first to go against the first natural impulse to resist this. So I accepted the current situation. I accepted that this was happening and this was a true reality. I accepted that this is a virus and yes, we are in a pandemic, and yes, the world is in a lockdown. And I accepted I had to rise up to the occasion.

The world may be overreacting, the virus may not be that lethal, and there could be a political agenda behind it and this could be a test for worse things to come. But why should I engage in all these views?

My rebellion was then against all the conspiracies and unsettling views that were out there. You see, my wife and I don't watch television. We do not watch the news. We haven't watched a full news program for over seven years now. But the social media posts were baits that both my wife and I got hooked on for a few days. We were bombarded with end-time prophecies, doom time videos, and scary, biblically unfounded outlooks.

So we decided to stop watching the nonsense that was out there and only stick to limited announcements made by credible sources such as our prime minister and our state premier. It had to be radical and quite against the new church trend that was looking for something that wasn't there.

The challenge was now to also guide the people in our churches to adapt to the "new normal" and to encourage them to cooperate and not let themselves be dragged down to drown in this sea of uncertainty and despair. This was confrontational. They were caught up in so many conspiracies evidently seen in their social media postings and through the materials shared on various group platforms.

Let me tell you that they did not appreciate my correction to simply accept things as they are. And yet, in this season we are called to lead. This is a responsibility we cannot ignore, nor put on the back burner. God is calling us to lead His church through this pandemic, and we are to rise up to this responsibility and do it well.

The conscious choice to *accept* the situation we were going through as it is, brought a state of assurance, rest, and hope in the Lord to us and to those who pushed ahead with it.

Living Abundantly in Every Situation

I treasure immensely the wisdom of the apostle Paul in Philippians 4:12. He said he knew how to live having almost nothing and also with having plenty. He knew how to enjoy a full stomach and an empty one. How did he know this? How could he adjust so easily? How could he accept things so fluidly? He said, he learned the secret. What secret? The secret of living in every situation. The acceptance to adapt to every situation. Rather than opposing what he was going through, he accepted it. He went on with it and knew that it would pass. That gave him the lenses to see the lesson in every situation.

Why do we resist the current situation? It is because we cannot control it. We like a high level of certainty and predictability. And at the same time we also like the thrill of some uncertainty and variety. But we like these balanced in a healthy tension. As soon as they are not, as it is with the coronavirus pandemic, we stress out. That stress brings anxiety, fear, and hopelessnes. To *accept* means to *not worry*.

Worry Is Not the Answer

It makes sense to look at Jesus' perspective on the subject of worry.

> *Therefore I tell you, do not be anxious about your life, what you will eat or what you will drink, nor about your body, what you will put on. Is not life more than food, and the body more than clothing? Look at the birds of the air: they neither sow nor reap nor gather into barns, and yet your heavenly Father feeds them. Are you not of more value than they? And which of you by being anxious can add a single hour to his span of life?* (Matthew 6:25-27)

> *For the Gentiles seek after all these things, and your heavenly Father knows that you need them all* (Matthew 6:32).

What is the Lord Jesus saying? We'll break it down to get a clear grasp of His take on how to deal with this.

1. Do not be anxious about your life. In other words, *do not worry*. Is this a suggestion or a command? It is a *command* from the very mouth of Jesus. If I do not obey His command, it means I am sinning against Him. It is therefore *illegal* for me to worry or be anxious about my life.

Also, Jesus cannot command us to do something we cannot do. If He is commanding us, this means that we can do it and we have to do it. It's a choice. To worry is a choice. And He is saying, *choose not to worry.*

Is this against the common trend? Absolutely.

2. Learn from the birds. I love how the Lord offers us a healthy perspective. He's saying that most of our worries have to do with our primary needs of food, clothing, and basic necessities.

He says, look at the birds. Why the birds? Because they are everywhere. You will see them in most places and they will speak to you of this verse. Every time you hear or see birds, you will be *reminded* of this verse. It is to help us remember that He provides for them, and for us. They are in His daily care—and so are we.

Where are the birds? In the air. Up. When the tendency to worry comes, Jesus is inviting us to *look up,* to lift our eyes and see that our help and provision comes from the Lord, the Creator of this world (Psalm 121:1-2). Accept this.

3. You are valuable in the eyes of God. Jesus wants us to see ourselves as He sees us, God's precious possession. We are more valuable than birds. We are His children (1 John 3:1). He gave us the value of His Son who died instead of us. And if He looks after the birds who have little value, will He not care for us who are His children? Let's accept our identity in Christ and His fatherly provision.

4. Worry does no good. The lesson the Lord is giving us here is profound and worth soul searching. What can you do by worrying? It's a really challenging question. What can you achieve by being anxious? Do you not see that this is outside your control? Why do you aim to control the things you cannot? Can you extend your life by worrying? Can you add an extra moment to your life?

We cannot. We have no control. So, worry is not the path that leads us to our desired solution or destiny. Worry is not the way. Worry says that God cannot be God over a situation. It takes away the sovereignty of God. Worry will keep us up at night and unsettle us throughout the day. Worry brings darkness in our mind, apathy in our behavior, and eventually will cripple us.

I heard a story once of an elderly lady who said, "I had many problems in my life, and most of them never happened." Her problems were all in her mind. Worries.

Personally, this lady's conclusion has given me healthy lenses throughout the past ten years or so since I heard it. My take on this is simple, if I can do something about the situation positively, I do it, and if I cannot, I will not worry about it. In fact, according to Jesus' teaching, it is illegal for me to worry about it.

The Secret of God's Provision

Now I am coming back to the apostle Paul who was so open to giving away vital life secrets. He gives us the secret to his contentment:

> *Not that I am speaking of being in need, for I **have learned** in whatever situation I am to be content. I know how to be brought low, and I know how to abound. In any and every circumstance, **I have learned the secret** of facing plenty and hunger, abundance and need. **I can do all things through him who strengthens me*** (Philippians 4:11-13).

Paul learned to be *content*. He learned to get along with humble means and also with prosperity, with facing hunger and with having plenty, with facing need and having abundance. How did he do that? He learned to rely on God's *provision*.

Instead of complaining, Paul adapted, he embraced the process, and he knew he could endure. He knew his source of strength. He lived according to his convictions, not conditions. He has learned that Christ's power, purpose, and provision are sufficient for every situation. That is why he could say, *"I can do all things through [God] who strengthens me"* (Philippians 4:13).

When the apostle Paul wrote to the church in Rome, he emphasized that the greatest provision God made for us was His Son, Jesus, and everything else is summed up in this provision: *"He who did not spare his own Son but gave him up for us all, how will he not also with him graciously give us all things?"* (Romans 8:32).

We have an opportunity to go through this pandemic relying on God's provision. Yes, this is an opportunity, because most of us are rarely faced with hunger and basic needs. It is a fresh perspective to learn contentment, gratitude, and reliance on God.

Learning the Secret of Gratitude

When the apostle Paul wrote about being content, he revealed that his demands and expectations were not high. When these are not high, they are easily met. What was the secret of his contentment? He was full of *gratitude*.

Paul told the Colossian church to let Christ's peace *rule* in their hearts, and to be *thankful* (Colossians 3:15). He said that he always thanked the Lord for them (Colossians 1:3). He also wrote to the church in Thessalonica to give thanks to God in everything (1 Thessalonians 5:18).

In fact, Paul uses the word "thanks" twenty-four times in his writings, the word "thank" eleven times, and "thanksgiving(s)" eight times. Adding all other variants of thankfulness together, there are *forty-nine* occurrences of proclaimed gratitude either to God or to the people he wrote to. Gratitude pulsed through his veins.

What is also beautiful about Paul's thankful writing is the adverbs he uses. He was thanking God *always* (1 Corinthians 1:4), for *everything, especially, without ceasing,* and even on people's *behalf.*

It is no wonder the "giving thanks psalm" exhorts us to, *"Enter his gates with thanksgiving, and his courts with praise! Give thanks to him; bless his name!"* (Psalm 100:4). When we learn to look at what we already have and who we already are we cannot hide how grateful and thankful we must be.

If you are a pastor, let me give you a coaching life hack here. If we can shift our people into a heart full of gratitude, it is one of the greatest renewals they can experience in their lives. This shift alone can help them rise above the current situation. Encouraging them to list or journal the things they are grateful for will change their mindset and help them overcome all the negativity surrounding them. And in Christ, we have a lot to be grateful for.

ONE APPLICATION

So, let me ask you these two questions:

1. What is the one thing you will do personally to deal with the current challenge?

2. And what is the one thing you will do for your church to assist in stepping up to the current coronavirus challenge?

CHAPTER 2

REVIEW YOUR QUESTIONS

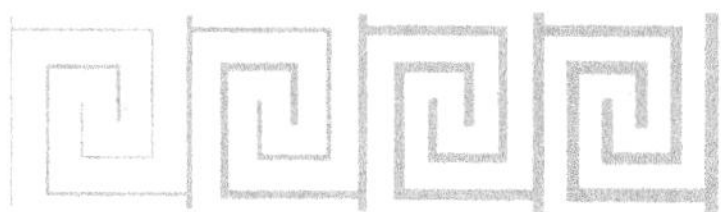

He [Jesus] *said to them, "But who do you say that I am?"*

—Matthew 16:15

The Challenges

→ *The world is asking plenty of questions at the moment.*

→ *It is a time of inquiry for the church, too.*

→ *Where is the church positioned regarding questions being asked?*

→ *Do we need answers or better questions?*

All around us at the moment people are asking questions. Both Christians and non-Christians have inquiries going through their minds and in their conversations with others. The door for some deep and meaningful investigations has been opened widely.

Einstein, who never stopped questioning, said: "If I had an hour to solve a problem and my life depended on the answer, I would spend the first fifty-five minutes figuring out the proper questions to ask. For if I knew the proper questions, I could solve the problem in less than five minutes."

The coronavirus lockdown is forcing the church to ask itself some unavoidable questions. The first temptation is to provide answers. We have been pretty good at providing answers for a long time, but not so good at asking questions. The reality is that right now we do not need answers. We need *better questions* to engage with the current situation.

I strongly believe that it's time for the church to *ask* these better questions. It's a lesson we cannot ignore. We must have some serious conversations about the current state of the church, how it is positioned in society, and what the future holds.

It is obvious that the church was not prepared for this worldwide health crisis. There were very few prophetic words about the coming pandemic and about the impact it would have on every sphere of every society, including religion. No one predicted we would be instantly locked out of our church buildings. It caught us unaware and unprepared.

What were we doing leading into this season? Let's challenge ourselves! Let's challenge our thinking! Let's challenge our activity! Let's challenge our direction! Let's inquire! Let's ask ourselves some real questions!

My daily activity is question based. I am an emotional intelligence coach as much as I am a pastor—and my job is to frame questions. These questions need to enable my clients to engage in a journey of discovery, deep inquest, and awareness. Questions are key to everything I do. And people pay to be asked tough questions and to be guided through the process of finding answers. The goal is not just to get to the bottom of the matter. There are beautiful discoveries found at every turn on the journey; and the process itself provides invaluable lessons for both the client and the coach.

Today's endless questions bring us back to Jesus. The Gospels are full of questions Jesus asked. He was the best coach who ever walked the face of the earth and His 307 Gospel questions give us unrivaled lessons.

How Did Jesus Frame His Questions?

Jesus was the best at asking thought-provoking, open questions for which most were not prepared. He *engaged through asking.* He was the Master of questions. He expertly *dug deep* into reality to produce both *self-awareness* and *God-awareness* in those with whom He spoke.

Jesus was guiding people into the depths of who they were. And He was rather ruthless about getting to the heart of people. Through His questions, He revealed who the Father was and also who they were.

Here are some vivid examples of Jesus' questions:

- "Who do you say that I am?" (Matthew 16:15, to His disciples)

- "Why do you call me good?" (Luke 18:19, to the young rich ruler)

- "What do you want me to do for you?" (Luke 18:41, to the blind beggar)

- "What are you seeking?" (John 1:38, to the two disciples)

- "Do you want to be healed?" (John 5:6, to the invalid at the Pool of Bethesda)

Our Questions Compared to His

Our tendency is to ask questions for *information.* Jesus asked questions that provoked *transformation.*

Our leaning is to ask questions for *answers*. Jesus asked questions for *awareness*.

Our questions demand *predictability*. Jesus asked questions for *curiosity*.

Our propensity is to ask questions for *comforting*. Jesus asked questions for *confrontation*.

The *invitation* and *challenge* is to learn of Him. Jesus invites us to ask ourselves questions that confront our thought process, our preconceptions, our conditioning, our assumptions, our judgments, and our beliefs. And this invitation is to do this in light of His perspective on every matter. This plays with our thinking. This makes us vulnerable. This makes us authentic.

What if Jesus is drawing us back into a time of examining ourselves with tough questions that reveal our hearts, the hidden reality of who we are? What if through this situation He is preparing us to engage with others in meaningful, soul-searching conversations that begin with rightly framed questions?

What We Learn from Jesus' Questions

1. Jesus' questions were real-life questions. His questions were specific, particular, and detailed. He wanted to deal with the broken-down details. His questions were not shallow, not about chit chat, not idle, and not abstract. They were somewhat uncomfortable and penetrated deeply. They were bold.

As people are searching for meaning and answers today, the church has an opportunity to get real and ask deep, soul-searching questions for itself and for those it serves in the community. Theology is great, doctrines are important, but today we have an opportunity to go into deep life matters as the soil has been prepared for us. People are not only questioning. They are also *listening* and are ready to *receive*. We need to be bold in our approach and go for it. They are searching for real life meaning, and for far too long we have given them a diluted, shallow gospel. It's time to get real!

2. Jesus' questions brought connection. His questions were personal encounters for Him. He knew that He may only get *one chance* with them and He got *personal.*

Nobody forgot an encounter with Jesus. He called people by name, communicating intimacy. He spoke to women, which was against the culture of the day. He questioned people's thinking, especially the religious people of the day. He did not leave anyone as He found them. He stirred them up and they had to jump off the fence, take a side, decide, and make a shift.

His communication through questions was aided by *eye contact* (Mark 10:21, Jesus looks at the rich young ruler and loves him), *body language* (John 8:8, Jesus bent down to write on the ground, restoring the woman caught in adultery), and *touch* (Matthew 8:3, Jesus touches the leper and heals him).

With the directive of social distancing today, people need connection more than ever. Are we *personal* enough to interact with people in a meaningful way?

3. Jesus' questions were full of compassion. His connection with people was characterized by a deep concern and often, gentle love. Jesus was present with them and was curious about their situation. He was questioning to understand, not to respond.

Jesus' presence brought comfort, healing, and kindness. His words were full of grace (Luke 4:22). He was a Friend of sinners (Matthew 11:19). And all these led the listeners to repentance.

We are inevitably instructed to be good listeners. Because of the pandemic, the whole world needs a listening ear and lots of compassion and empathy. People are not looking for solutions or a fix. They are looking for love and connection.

Our questions today can bring friendship and connection, comfort and healing, words of grace and kindness. Let's review our questions and learn to ask better ones, more meaningful ones, and much deeper ones.

4. Jesus' questions went deep to go high. Look at Jesus in His discussion with the rich young man in Mark 10:17-22:

> *And as he was setting out on his journey, a man ran up and knelt before him and asked him, "Good Teacher, what must I do to inherit eternal life?" And Jesus said to him, **"Why do you call me good?** No one is good except God alone. You know the commandments: 'Do not murder, Do not commit adultery, Do not steal, Do not bear false witness, Do not defraud, Honor your father and mother.'" And he said to him, "Teacher, all these I have kept from my youth." And Jesus, looking at him, loved him, and said to him, **"You lack one thing:** go, sell all that you have and give to the poor, and you will have treasure in heaven; and come, follow me." Disheartened by the saying, he went away sorrowful, for he had great possessions.*

The young man's first question was a genuine inquiry into how he can inherit eternal life. Most people would have given him something like the "Four Steps to Salvation." We'd go high. Jesus goes deep, and in essence says, "Did you just call Me good? Why do you call Me good? You know that only God is good, so what are you saying? Are you saying that I am God? If so, how are you honoring God? How are you obeying His commands?"

Wow! Look at the depth of that conversation from the word, go. Look at the stir, the depth, the confrontation, the possibilities. Look where this is going!

Obviously this story does not have a happy ending. It is, in fact, one of the saddest stories in the Gospels. It shows that someone can encounter the love of Jesus, face to face, eyes to eyes, and yet still walk away disheartened.

But the point here is that Jesus went deep instantly, to go to his heart, to go high. And as soon as He went deep, the young man had to make a choice. Jesus did not leave him where He found him. He had to either accept Christ and follow Him, or turn his back on Him.

Can you see how meaningless and shallow our conversations can be compared to this example?

It's time to review our questions. It's time to realize that we have an unmatched opportunity in this time to go deep. People are now ready. Both in our private conversations and in our churches, it's time to ask tough questions about life, about the meaning of life, about the gospel, about Christ, about salvation.

In the current world full of uncertainty, I see a massive open door. The search for truth has never been such priority in the world as it is now. We live in a world full of lies; and even though this has always been the case, now with this pandemic, we are all affected. Until now the effect was not felt as we, overall, had it pretty good.

The lack of genuine information compounded by the brainwashing of the media gets people even more stirred up to seek answers in their search for truth, meaning, and purpose. This gives us a clear connection point with anyone we talk to. By simply asking a few questions we can remove layers and get to the heart of the matter quite quickly. We can now go deep rather fast. Our aim is to go high, but our way there is by going deep—just like Jesus did.

ONE APPLICATION

1. What have you learned through reading this chapter, and what will you personally implement?

2. What is the one thing your church can apply from this chapter?

CHAPTER 3

RESTORE JESUS AS THE MASTER BUILDER

And I tell you, you are Peter, and on this rock I will build my church, and the gates of hell shall not prevail against it.

—Matthew 16:18

The Challenges

→ *We have been busy building the church.*

→ *The church we built is so dependent on buildings.*

→ *The church needs to redefine who it is and who is building it.*

→ *What is the role of Christ in today's churches?*

One of the most vital lessons we are to learn in this time has to do with who Christ is for the church and what role does He play in church's existence, growth, and development. There are some tough questions we need to ask ourselves in this time of reflection.

- How healthy is our church today?

- What are we focused on?

- What are we building toward?

- Where does our energy go?
- What is the vision worked out in our church at the moment? (Not the one on our website.)

Then we should go further in our quest and inquire about the church and its mission. Have you ever wondered why the church operates the way it does? Did you ever ask yourself, *Why are there so many denominations, movements—and why do churches look so different from one another both in practices and doctrines?*

Over the last century, and more so in recent history, we have been busy building our churches and ministries. We are planting churches more than ever before, we are buying buildings (and in some places selling them), we are building up ministries and we push for growth, development, and expansion.

What have we been missing? We've missed the very first notion that Jesus spoke about. *Jesus is building His church,* not us. He is the *Master Builder!* Yet we seem to overlook this fact. We may be too used to this Scripture to allow it to do its work in us afresh.

"I Will Build My Church"

Jesus asked His disciples who they thought He was, what was His identity (Matthew 16:13-16). Simon Peter's reply is the foundational truth of the church: *"You are the Christ, the Son of the living God."* Jesus' response gives us the blueprint for the church, saying, *"...I will build my church..."* (Matthew 16:17-19).

The tendency for church leaders is to build churches. We often reference God's church as *my church* or *our church*. We are busy creating systems, programs, hierarchy, strategies, ministries, projects, and development programs, which preoccupies most of our time and energy.

Getting the Sunday "event" spot-on is our main focus, and we spend *most of our energy* on that. I reflected on this reality while pastoring a church with a generous annual budget of just over $1 million, and realized that our Sunday service was central to everything we did. All was geared toward that Sunday expression. Breaking it down financially, our Sunday "show" cost close to $20,000. This was an eye opener! Were we a church or an event organization?

Jesus laid His foundation on how the church would be built.

1. *Jesus will build it.* He is the Founder, the Initiator, the Pioneer, the Designer, the Architect, and also the *Master Builder*. This is *His business* per say, not ours. We have began doing His work and avoided ours. We engage in doing His part, ignoring ours. We thought we could do it better than He could, so we went on and did it. Then after we did it, we asked Him to bless it.

Consider the following statement of the apostle Paul who brings the church's identity in Christ:

> *And he* [Jesus] *put all things under his feet and gave him as head over all things to the church, which is his body, the fullness of **him who fills all in all*** (Ephesians 1:22-23).

2. *The church is Christ's.* He is the *Head* of His church. The head is not the pastor, the minister, the reverend, or the pope. This is the reason why the Reformers denied the authority of the papal office. It took away Christ's rule over the church. The church is not a democracy as many believe in the West. It is a Christocracy—Christ is the Head of the church.

The church was to carry the vision of the Head and the plans of the Head to achieve the final end goal for the church. Christ was to fill it all in all as He is the Head and the true Master Builder (Ephesians 1:23).

If we are the ones building Christ's church, we cannot achieve the end goal for the church. And that end goal is twofold: 1) to be His earthly body now and 2) His bride upon His return.

The church belongs to Him. I reiterate this as we need to really get it. The church is His. And He is the One building it. He is building it in a way that no one, not even the gates of hell can take it down. Why has the church survived over the centuries even though it went through so much opposition and persecution? Because it belongs to Jesus, and He is actively looking after it and building it.

3. *The church is not a building, nor a project.* The church is a *people*. Where these people meet and how they meet is irrelevant. Whether they have a building or not is irrelevant. *The church is a body brought to life in Christ.* The Lord is restoring each life, each dead rock into a *living stone* to form His body, the church. How does He do this? He does it by ripping down the gates of hell that hold every human heart in hell-destined sin (Matthew 16:18).

4. *The church is Christ's body.* The living stones of all believers form His body. Yes, there is a role for us to play, but only as His body. He is the Head and believers are active members in His body (1 Corinthians 12:27).

5. *We are the church, God's holy temple.* Yes, you and I are the church and there's an active role for us in Christ's church. Our role is to preach the gospel, to testify of Jesus, to make disciples, to serve, to care, to reach out in love, and to advance God's Kingdom. But isn't this what the church does, you may ask? Yes, all these are the workings of the church. But the building up of the church is a supernatural, God-mastered result of all of these expressions.

When we are busy doing the work of the ministry that God has called us to do, Jesus is building His church. The one Spirit who dwells in believers unites all believers into a dwelling place of God. We become God's temple both at the individual level and at the church level. We are framing, in a way, the house of God. That is why the apostle Paul told the Corinthian church that they are the holy temple (1 Corinthians 3:17).

On This Rock

We know that for a building to stand, it must have first the *right foundation,* then the right structure. The foundation on which the Lord is building the church is not our mission statement, our vision statement, our movement's system, or our franchise plan.

Jesus told Peter that the rock or foundation on which He is building His church is the *testimony* that He is the Christ, the Messiah, the Son of the living God (Matthew 16:13-16). The foundation is Jesus and His gospel.

We need to come back to this rock all the time. We can never permit our churches to veer away from this foundational truth, especially in a time of crisis such as the coronavirus pandemic. Why? Because people need a solid rock to stand on! They need an absolute Truth that brings them certainty, assurance, and security. And that solid rock of who Jesus is has proven to be so strong that it held the church alive and the believers going throughout the centuries, no matter what challenges they went through, including famine, persecution, and yes, pandemics.

This reaffirms that Christ has placed His church on a solid rock that *will withstand* the current lockdown. Even though church *buildings* are shut at the moment, the *church* is thriving in homes. Why? Because church is built on the *testimony of Jesus,* His gospel.

The current situation refreshes in our hearts and in our minds the timeless truth that the testimony of Jesus is the foundation to all we do, and that Christ is the Master Builder of His church.

ONE APPLICATION

1. What is the one shift this chapter is making in your life right now?

2. What is the one shift for your church you will take on?

CHAPTER 4

RESETTING TRUE FELLOWSHIP

*They devoted themselves to the apostles' **teaching** and to the **fellowship**, to the **breaking of bread** and the **prayers**.*

—Acts 2:42

The Challenges

→ *Churches today are generally driven by programs or events.*

→ *Limited services means limited fellowship.*

→ *Church fellowship is generally shallow.*

→ *Biblical fellowship needs to be a priority.*

I love how the book of Acts unpacks the early days of the church, and I refer to their unity, inclusiveness, care for one another, and their exemplary practices. I, as other pastors, have gone further and adopted some of these in our church's manifesto. Our church has even embraced the four pillars of Acts 2:42 as the way of doing church, as the working out of our faith.

Many churches take these four practices and make every effort to apply them in the church family. What we are missing though, is the *devotion* part, the continuity aspect, the steadfast embracing, the perseverance. And this has signaled a red flag during the coronavirus lockdown.

When we were meeting in church buildings, we knew how to do this or at least we thought we knew. We knew how to listen to the apostles' teachings and we knew how to teach. We thought we knew how to do fellowship, how to break bread, and how to pray. In fact, we already had it all planned out. It was almost predictable. And sadly, we thought we were pretty good at it.

The current situation does not give churches the opportunity to come together in a building to apply these the way we used to. And I thank the Lord for that.

You see, two out of the four practices of the early church (fellowship and breaking of bread) had to do with *intimate* fellowship. If we were to consider them as proportions of time, half of their time together was about fellowship. I believe this highlights how important and close their connection in fellowship was.

The Myth of Self-Fellowship

A strange idea has crept into the church in our modern times that you can walk your Christian walk by yourself, that it's just between you and God, and as long as you have fellowship with God, all is good.

Well, your faith journey does have an individual aspect to it; however, it has a communal aspect just as much, in fact a lot more. For fellowship, there has to be at least two or three people coming together. I believe that being forced into our homes during this time, we can really appreciate that fellowship is not an individual pursuit.

How many believers have visited another church hoping that no one would interact with us? We made sure we arrived just after it started, so we don't have to meet anyone before the service and have to answer questions. We looked for a place at the back of the sanctuary, as far back as possible, but without looking too out of place on the back row. We ensured that there was enough social distancing on either side of us by placing our Bible, phone, or bag on the seats.

We hoped that the lights were off so no one could see us or recognize us. And then we sat quietly, enjoying the connection with God in an individual way, yet being part of a larger assembly. We talked ourselves into "This is between me and God" way of worshipping. At the end of the service we either sneaked out at the final prayer, or shot straight out afterward to avoid contact with anyone. And if someone asked us afterward how it was at church that morning, we would define it as an excellent time with the Lord. *That* is not fellowship!

We also miss social interactions during this lockdown and we probably miss these more than church interactions. It can be very attractive to meet up with other believers for playing a game of football, taking a walk, having coffee, watching sport, and still not going anywhere deep in our discussion or relational connection. This is shallow fellowship, a form of a fellowship fix at best.

The Fellowship Fix

In a modern-day believer's mind, fellowship means going to a church building for service on Sunday morning, shaking hands, or hugging with the welcoming team (not so much now), exchanging a couple of helloes mainly through acknowledging smiles, finding a seat not too close to the front, entering the time of singing, maybe prayer, the offering, and in some cases, even joining in the "meet and greet."

Then it's the announcements, the message, a call to prayer at the end, and some sort of interaction after the service. This could include some more helloes with overrated smiles, a cup of tea or coffee and some biscuits, and some shallow conversation exchanges with someone known or someone freshly met.

And there's the fellowship fix for the week.

In some cases there's a midweek prayer or Bible study get together where the connection can get deeper, but this can take time and there is usually a great deal of resistance to open conversations, not to mention the fact that only a small percentage of people actually show up. Once a month the church serves communion and occasionally some sort of get together around tables.

Years go by and even though the church attendance is good, tithes are observed, and people seem generally content, no one knows what goes on in people's lives until trouble hits and by then it is a bit too late to provide rescue. We can be easily disillusioned into thinking that the way we are doing fellowship is sufficient for the general church members.

The fellowship fix is limited mainly to church participation and practised as a few handshakes, hugs, ministry activity, sitting together in an auditorium, looking at each other (visual fellowship), and the occasional coffee or tea after the service.

And now because of the lockdown we're in trouble as we can't even get this *fix*. We cannot meet in the church buildings for a while and as such, we don't have practical ways of fellowship. Social distancing was in our churches long before it even became a worldwide issue. Notice I wrote *social distancing*, not *physical distancing*.

This was an oversight that needs correction. I believe God is allowing this to happen *for* the church—not just *to* the church—to reset and engage in true fellowship.

Resetting Fellowship

In the New Testament, *koinonia* signifies having a share in something, or sharing with someone in something, or participating in something or with someone. It is a mutual bond developed with Christ that places us in a *deep* and *eternal relationship* with one another.

In 1 Corinthians 10:16, the apostle Paul talks about fellowship as being *a participation in the bread and blood of Christ,* meaning that we share in what Jesus did for us on the cross.

In 2 Corinthians 8:4, the Macedonians wanted to *share in the ministry to the saints* by sending financial aid to the poor in Jerusalem.

The apostle Paul wanted to have a share (fellowship) in the sufferings of Christ (Philippians 3:10), to *participate with him in suffering* for the gospel.

True fellowship means *partnering* with God and one another in working out our salvation. It is spending intentional time with God and other believers. It is a *common enjoyment* that Christians have and experience. It is a process of building each other up, and a time of encouragement and exhortation to holy living. It means caring for one another and bearing one another's burdens. True fellowship is a *ministry to one another.*

There are 100 "one another's" in the New Testament. Half of those are directed to the church. Take your time to search for them and read them. It will reframe fellowship in your mind and in your heart. We need this as Christians.

Fellowship conveys the *nature* and *reality* of the Christian expression. Believers have fellowship with God in the New Covenant established by Jesus Christ, and with one another. There is a *new reality* about the Christian life that many are yet to embrace. It is a real and practical sharing of Jesus' life. In 1 John 1:3-6 we see the practical reality of our fellowship with God—walking in the light of God's Word.

When we read of the early church giving themselves to fellowship, we begin to understand that the way they did it was *life on life*. No one was in need; no one was left out. They had everything in common (Acts 2:44). They came into agreement and into one accord (Acts 2:46).

The church is invited to return to true fellowship and to do life on life. It is invited to get a bit messy, a bit uncomfortable, a bit more real. It is an invitation to vulnerability, to openness, to togetherness, to unity, and to partnership.

I believe the Lord wants to reestablish a few vital practices and realities that were either lost or overlooked by our modern church. And when it comes to fellowship, here's a short list to begin with:

1. Identify each other as brothers and sisters and call each other brothers and sisters. In Matthew 12:48-50, Jesus calls those who do the will of God His *brothers* and *sisters*. By simply returning to this godly practice, there will be a constant reminder of our relational *identity*.

Brothers and sisters forgive each other. They have a lifetime covenantal relationship. They help and care for each other. They have each other's back. We are all born of God (1 John 4:7) who is our Father, and we inherit His supernatural nature, the DNA of godly love. I strongly believe that this will unlock a divine relational grace over us.

2. Engage in deep, life-on-life relationships. In today's modern world we live more and more segregated lives. Deep conversations are rare and the element of trust bothers us. We are careful not to expose ourselves so we do not get hurt, mainly emotionally. The temptation is to avoid deep and meaningful relationships.

It's time to be *truly relational!* It's time to look to other's interests (Philippians 2:4). It is time to be honest with ourselves and remove the veil that hides us. It is time to say things that will keep each other believing. It is time to allow others to speak into our lives and for us to have the love and freedom to do the same. It is time to be strong through vulnerability.

The apostle John highlights how love is to be manifested in relationships: *"There is no fear in love, but perfect love drives out fear. For fear has to do with punishment, and whoever fears has not been perfected in love"* (1 John 4:18).

Life on life means calling one another, visiting one another, talking deeply with one another, praying with each other, helping one another, encouraging one another, studying the Word together, going for walks, correcting one another, and doing life together. Yes, we need to be in each other's face more often, a bit messier, and more intentional.

Life on life means looking after each other. It means helping one another work out their salvation. Why are so many falling away from the faith today? Why do so many young people drift away from God? Why are there so many people lost today even though they once confessed Jesus as their Lord? It may be because there was no one looking out for them. It may be because they never engaged in true and meaningful relationships.

Notice how in the following Scripture passage we have a *responsibility* for exhorting one another and looking after each other, daily.

> ***See to it***, *brothers and sisters, that none of you has a sinful, unbelieving heart that turns away from the living God. But encourage one another daily, as long as it is called "Today," so that none of you may be hardened by sin's deceitfulness* (Hebrews 3:12-13 NIV).

Two vital imperatives must be noticed here. The first is, "*See to it.*" Take care and do it. The second is, "*encourage one another.*" If we all do this in true fellowship with one another, a situation like the coronavirus isolation will have little or no impact on the church when it comes to fellowship.

I believe the Lord is restoring the relational, life-on-life priority to the church in this time. I believe God wants us to go deep before we go wide. I believe the church has missed this, especially in the West where our lives are so segregated. The Lord is stirring in us in this time a longing for deep and meaningful fellowship. Praise God for this!

3. Prioritizing fellowship. For the early church, fellowship was a constant priority. They devoted themselves to this, daily. Even the Lord's Supper was a daily celebration; that's what the Lord intended it to be, a remembrance that honored Him every time His disciples came together. They embraced fellowship as a constant reminder of their identity in Christ and as a constant working out of their faith in Him.

Faith requires perseverance. One way for perseverance to be accomplished is through prioritizing constant fellowship. If we look at the five dynamics of the falling away from God in Hebrews 3:12-13, we see that we have a job to prevent these from happening. The sinful heart (v.12), unbelief (v.12), hardness (v.13), sin (v.13) and sin's deceitfulness (v.13) are the factors that cause turning away from God.

When we have fellowship we can speak of and address all these aspects as they happen, not after they happened. In fellowship we dig deep into what goes on in the heart; and as we have a safe place to explore that, we have the possibility to exhort and encourage one another to persevere in faith.

You may ask, why is this important. I understand that most of our interchanges as Christians are not crisis or sin based, but every one of them counts for eternity. You see, we either strengthen our brothers and sisters in their faith, or weaken them. We are either building them up, or unfortunately dragging them down. We are either devoted to one another or working against one another. That is why true fellowship requires devotion.

ONE APPLICATION

1. What is a *personal* application you will implement from this lesson?

2. What is a *church* application you will take on from this lesson?

CHAPTER 5

REBUILD THE HOME CHURCH

For where two or three are gathered in my name,
there am I among them.

—Matthew 18:20

The Challenges

→ *The church cannot meet in buildings nor in large assemblies.*

→ *The church has not been taught how to meet in homes.*

→ *The priesthood of all believers is an accepted principle, but rarely practised.*

→ *The home church needs rebuilding.*

The coronavirus pandemic has impacted churches worldwide in unprecedented ways. Never before have we had a full world lockdown of churches. To many church-going people, this was shocking and frightening bad news; while to others, it was a welcomed refreshing prospect.

How can the same situation bring such divided views? Many saw this as an attack on the church and became hurt by it. Others saw the opportunity to reestablish something that was lost over the millennia, the house church. The church is coming back *home!*

This has prompted us to revisit the early church and how they did church in their homes. For some this may seem like a step backward, but I do not think it is. I believe house churches needed to be restored. And God is using the current world crisis to realign our families and our homes to be what we were meant to be from the beginning. And then the Sunday celebration gathering will be renewed and refreshed.

I welcome the current challenge, and I pray that you do as well. We were too comfortable for too long. We did church, but we were not always the church. We came to church, sat in our pews, sang, prayed, tithed, listened to the preaching, even got involved in some ministry—and this was our routine Sunday way of doing church. It was predictable, unchallenging, easily performed, and guilt satisfying.

Church is so much more than what we are used to during our Sunday service. And because we have limited it to a Sunday corporate expression, we have been missing so much of the components that should make the church a living organism, thriving and growing in every situation and in every home.

Back to Where Church Began—in Homes

The early church was an *organic* entity. It was the living, breathing body of Christ revealing Christ to the world. Believers were meeting in homes, and every person was part of all that was happening. It was a natural and spontaneous Spirit-filled life manifesting itself in a group of people who began to simply gather together to honor Christ.

The first century church was simple, genuine, and inclusive. There was a corporate element in the temple and an intimate expression in their homes.

And day by day, attending the temple together and breaking bread in their homes, they received their food with glad and generous hearts (Acts 2:46).

Church was part of their daily living, not a Sunday ritual. They shared meals together daily, took the Lord's Supper daily, and shared life with one another. There was an organized part to it, but most of it was organic. They were the church—and the result was astounding:

*So the church throughout all Judea and Galilee and Samaria had **peace** and was being **built up**. And walking in the **fear** of the Lord and in the **comfort** of the Holy Spirit, it **multiplied** (Acts 9:31).*

1. They were multiplying. Not growing in our way of thinking. From the beginning God told Adam and Eve to be fruitful and *multiply* (Genesis 1:28). We should not focus on growing churches but we are to *multiply* them.

The only way this can happen in a biblical way is to do it in the homes first, at the family level. There was a church in *every* Christian home. The multiplication was instant as a new family came to Christ. This is a valuable lesson the Lord is teaching us again.

2. They were maturing. The church had *peace* and was being *built up*. They lived in *fear* of the Lord. Their *comfort* was in the Holy Spirit. This spells *maturity*. These people were not church members. They were *disciples*, disciples of Jesus—not of the church and not of a particular leader.

The early church only made *disciples*. There were no other forms of believers. We need to come back to this spiritual truth of making disciples, *mature followers of Jesus*. Our churches are full of members, but we lack disciples. Discipleship takes time and it cannot be done in the institutionalized church model. This is done in homes as we do life together throughout the week. We are forced to take a good look at this and engage in discipleship making as an organic way of our Christian life.

3. They were serving. They were doing life together (church) with *gladness* and *generous hearts* (Acts 2:46). They were making sure everyone was included and lacked nothing. You can only enjoy peace and be built up when everyone has a glad attitude and a generous, servant heart. Life in the home is a *life of service.* Everyone plays a part in the life of the family and naturally in the organic home church.

4. They were family churches. Every *family* was a church as much as they welcomed others in their home church and more so than the way they participated in temple gatherings. We lost the idea of focusing on the *whole family* and preaching the gospel to the whole family. We forget that God created the family first—and that's where the blessing begins.

Our tendency is to focus on the individual, and that is why we have so many issues with the families in our churches. There's a fresh alignment that the Lord is doing here now. He is restoring the family unit.

Families that accept Christ are immediately a dwelling place of God. That's what the first century church focused on. They went from house to house and established home churches wherever they had an opening. In Acts 16:15 it was Lydia *and* her household; in Acts 16:33 the jailer *and* all his family; and in Acts 18:8 Crispus *and* everyone in his household. That is why the churches multiplied rapidly.

The Home Church Today

There has to be a natural and organic way of doing home church today. I am not advocating ditching your Sunday corporate expression. On the contrary, I believe we should first be the church in our homes, neighborhoods, and in our workplaces, and then come together in the wider body and celebrate in the larger gathering what the Lord has been doing in us as His church throughout the week.

The Lord is not asking us to have home church services to emulate the church programs in our homes. He wants us to be His church. He wants constant communion with our family. Worship, prayer, breaking of bread, and Bible study should be naturally done around the dinner table, in living rooms, in the car, and in our outdoor spaces.

This should become the *norm*. Fathers and mothers step up in their priesthood calling, children grow immersed in the daily celebration of Christ in their homes, and anyone who comes into their home encounters Jesus. This could be an area we have neglected in our churches. We have not properly equipped people, mothers and fathers in their priesthood (1 Peter 2:5,9).

The reformation that happened 500 years ago is still to reform some of our people, and some of our leaders. Do we believe in the priesthood of all believers? If we do, this must be proven by the way we engage in it and the way we release our folk to operate in this calling.

This should not be a chore and a burden on the family. It should be an *intentional priority* of doing life with Christ in the every day. There should be freedom to worship in the house, freedom to pray without ceasing, freedom to talk about and study spiritual matters, and freedom to enjoy the Lord's Supper together. As parents we are to model this.

Out of this identity as being the church at home, everyone in the family can love and minister to other families and everyone they encounter. The result is that the church will be multiplied in the homes; and when all these home churches come together on Sunday in the corporate gathering, there will be glorious celebrations! Sunday church will be different. They have to be. Let's not return to the old way of doing church just on Sunday. Let's be the church every day!

ONE APPLICATION

1. What is the lesson you're taking on for yourself to apply?

2. What is the applicable lesson for your church?

CHAPTER 6

REASSESS YOUR MOTIVES

You ask and do not receive, because you ask wrongly,
to spend it on your passions.

—James 4:3

The Challenges

→ *The church rarely looks at its motives.*

→ *The church has many leaders and followers with wrong motives.*

→ *The church is going through a time of sifting.*

→ *The church needs to reassess to whom it belongs.*

One of the first questions we get asked immediately after we introduce ourselves or are introduced to someone is what we do for a living. When I tell people I am a pastor, they immediately assume it must be so fulfilling. Not many people look at the ministry job as a moneymaking career or a profitable marketplace business. They relate to it as a calling, and sometimes they ask why I do it.

So recently I asked myself this very question. Why do I do it? What is my reason for doing ministry? What is my inner motive?

Am I doing it because I believe God asked me to do it? Am I in ministry because I want to be a leader or a preacher? Am I involved in this for the sake of saving my family? Am I trying to prove something to someone? Am I doing this for myself? Am I doing this for God?

What about the church I lead? What is the reason we do what we do? Why do we do church? And now that we cannot meet together, what are we to do? This will test us; it will test our motives and our core basis for doing what we do. It will expose our blind spots and our hidden attitudes. Only when we're tested can we get a clear view of where we are.

Do We Have the Right Motive?

There is a thought-provoking chapter in the book of James that may point to some issues in our churches, both within the church and also between the churches. How can we impact the world without doing an internal investigation as well?

What causes quarrels and what causes fights among you? Is it not this, that your passions are at war within you? You desire and do not have, so you murder. You covet and cannot obtain, so you fight and quarrel. You do not have, because you do not ask. You ask and do not receive, because you ask wrongly, to spend it on your passions. You adulterous people! Do you not know that friendship with the world is enmity with God? Therefore whoever wishes to be a friend of the world makes himself an enemy of God. Or do you suppose it is to no purpose that the Scripture says, "He yearns jealously over the spirit that he has made to dwell in us"? But he gives more grace. Therefore it says, "God opposes the proud but gives grace to the humble." Submit yourselves therefore to God. Resist the devil, and he will flee from you. Draw near to God, and he will draw near to you. Cleanse your hands, you sinners, and purify your hearts, you double-minded. Be wretched and mourn and weep. Let your laughter be turned to mourning and your joy to gloom. Humble yourselves before the Lord, and he will exalt you (James 4:1-10).

What is the problem in our churches at the moment? People? Divisions? Are we part of the problem? James asks us about our passions. What are we yearning? What do we burn inside for? Are these aligned with God or are they selfish? Are they at war within you?

What is the purpose of doing church?

- Is it *tradition?* We have to have church in every neighborhood for people to attend on Sundays.

- Is it *events?* It is important to have services that people can relate to and engage in.

- Is it *building* related? There has to be a building and around that we can build the whole ministry.

- Is it *feelings* based? Our community needs to feel loved and welcomed so we can usher them into a relationship with God.

What if all of these, no matter how great they are, do not have the right *motive* at heart? James provokes us to dig deep into the *desires of our hearts.* For whom and why are you spending all this energy, effort, and money? Is it not for *our* passions? Is it not for *ourselves?*

Aren't you going to church for yourself, for your family, and for securing your future? Aren't you committed to following the Lord so you don't end up in hell? Aren't you leading the church or a ministry as a call of God on your life? Aren't you a pastor or church leader because the community needs you, and God needs you?

What if all this church business is not really about us? What if our motives are wrong? What if our desires are selfish? What if our spending is not godly?

James tells us two reasons we don't have timely answers to the challenging questions of today.

1. We don't have because we don't ask (James 4:2). We ask to receive what we think we need. We do not know how to ask. We do not know how to align with God's will, on earth as it is in heaven. We ask God to bless what we are doing, not for us to do what He is blessing. We receive little because we have an earthly perspective instead of a heavenly perspective.

We don't dare ask for heavenly blessings because we are too entangled in needing earthly blessings. We are too focused on the tangible, of the here and now, and lose track of the eternal, things-of-above picture.

People came to Jesus asking for miracles, healings, and food. The challenging questions Jesus threw back at them always had to do with their motives. Did they want His blessings, or did they believe in Him?

We don't receive because we don't always ask Jesus to be the Lord. We generally ask Him to be our Provider, and not so much our Lord.

2. We don't have because we ask wrongly (James 4:3). We ask to receive for ourselves—even though we say our church. It is for us—for our passions, our vision, our purposes.

We want our service to be the best show in town. We want our team to be the most dynamic and gifted. We want our band to be the center stage of our celebration. We want our community services to be the talk of the town. We want our pastor to be the best communicator—not preacher—in the area. We want our building to be the newest and best decked out church this side of town. We want fame, which spells pride. And God opposes the proud.

Through all this, *God yearns jealously over the spirit that He has made to dwell in us.* He wants our spirit to connect and align with His Spirit. And He wants to reveal His heart and His motives to our spirit.

It's time to ask ourselves tough questions about our motives. It is time to reframe our questions to get to the bottom of this.

- What is the real reason and the real purpose for doing church?

- How pure are we in our thinking and in our hearts (James 4:8)?

- How honest are we with ourselves?

- How well do we forgive?

- How is our love for one another?

- Are we proud (James 4:6)?

Our Church or God's Church?

What is our view of the church we lead? Is it our church or God's church? I am not talking about what we say, I am talking about what we think down deep within, the meaning we give our thoughts and the unseen attitude we have.

If we truly believe that the church we pastor or serve belongs to God, our attitude and motives change. If not, we will feel the need to compare and compete with other churches and ministries. We will think it's all about us and our performance, and it isn't.

Unless you have the right motives, you will not fulfill God's assignment for you in His church. Speaking to pastors and church or ministries leaders for a moment, if you fear losing your people or your income during the coronavirus lockdown, you have the wrong understanding of church. If you have been using people for their services or their finances rather than caring for them, you have real reasons for concern. If your integrity is questionable, your ministry may not stand the test at hand.

Wanting your church to be strong, resilient, and growing is not a bad thing. It is noble and worthy of your passion. But if the purest motive in your leadership is not for people to come to Jesus, to be loved, forgiven, saved, and discipled, then you are doing a massive disfavor to God and to everyone you lead.

Let me give you a quick test. When it comes to your church, do you desire it to grow? If so, ask yourself why. Is it because of pride? You will say, no. Okay, but how do you feel when the church doesn't grow? Or better yet, how do you feel when it does? Maybe church growth is a deep motive you have, and that has become an unconscious idol to you. If success goes to your head when you grow and failure goes to your heart when you don't, your motives are wrong.

A leader with the right motives leads well regardless of the challenges faced, be it the coronavirus lockdown or some other challenge. A godly leader can lead in a time of crisis and in a time of success—and is humble enough to depend on God secured in personal identity and not performance.

Another temptation the coronavirus has brought to the surface is comparing ourselves and our churches with others. We are drawn in to see what others are doing and how we can compete. This leads to relational problems between churches, leaders, and even church members.

Again, is it our church or our ministry, or God's? When God looks at a city, how many churches does He see? He should see one church gathered in many places. Does He see that in your city? Are you contributing to the unity of the church in the city or to its division?

It starts with your deep desires for doing church. It begins with us—believers in the Lord, our heavenly Father.

Prepare for a season of real issues to come out of the woods during this period of uncertainty and lockdown. Families are stuck together and they have to sort out some of their relational issues. Their beneath-the-surface attitudes will be exposed. They will need guidance through this reassessment of motives.

Every area of ministry will undergo a test during the very season we are in and the season ahead. Keep your heart pure knowing something good is coming out of this no matter how uncomfortable and confronting it may be.

A Time of Sifting

Sifting is the process of separating the grain from the stalk and the chaff. It is not a pleasant action whether is done by hand or machinery. It is quite harsh for the wheat because it breaks it apart. The process separates the valuable portion from the worthless portion.

Jesus told Peter he would undergo a sifting. He said, *"Simon, Simon, behold, Satan demanded to have you, that he might sift you like wheat, but I have prayed for you that your faith may not fail. And when you have turned again, strengthen your brothers"* (Luke 22:31-32).

There was an attack of the devil on Peter because he was going against the kingdom of darkness. Jesus had just promised to build His church on Peter's testimony (Matthew 16:18). This sifting was going to produce abundant blessings in Peter, no matter how hard or uncomfortable it would be. And the Lord didn't just allow it to happen and then turn away. He prayed for Peter and for his faith to remain strong.

The trials and challenges we experience in the church life are used by God to sift us. They are tests. I believe the coronavirus is such a test. This period of history is a sifting period for the church, for leaders and for the people of our churches. Everyone will experience some sort of sifting in this time—wives, husbands, and children. It is natural to want a peaceful and comfortable life without any storms and turmoil. It is desirable to have glorious churches without problems or troubles. But the reality is we need to be tested. These trials purify us. Sifting does away with all the chaff and worthless part of us. Sifting works for us to get rid of all the toxic attitudes we may have harbored.

It is beautiful how Christ intercedes for Peter, and for us. He wants us to persevere in faith through this time of doubt and uncertainty. He wants us to remember His love and commitment to those He died to save. And He wants us to realize that He allows the sifting to test our faith. This process works for us not against us. It examines us and defines who we truly are inside. It goes deep to the core of our being to bring the best, or the worst, in us.

In my ministry here in Australia, I have lost some leaders during this period. They failed the test. The sifting took them out. Their motives were exposed and they couldn't get through this time. We lost some church people, too. I wanted to go after them, but the Lord told me that I am to go only after the lost sheep, not the stubborn sheep.

Hope Beyond Motives

There is hope though, even if the right motives are not always there. God can still work through some of the weaknesses we have in our churches. Look at the apostle Paul's perspective:

And most of the brothers, having become confident in the Lord by my imprisonment, are much more bold to speak the word without fear. Some indeed preach Christ from envy and rivalry, but others from good will. The latter do it out of love, knowing that I am put here for the defense of the gospel. The former proclaim Christ out of selfish ambition, not sincerely but thinking to afflict me in my imprisonment. What then? Only that in every way, whether in pretense or in truth, Christ is proclaimed, and in that I rejoice (Philippians 1:14-18).

Paul saw beyond the immaturity of wrong attitude. He was able to rejoice that the gospel was proclaimed even though some had wrong motives. He knew who he was ministering to and he was able to carry on his ministry with a pure heart regardless of what was going on around him.

What an amazing example apostle Paul is for us. Reassess your motives. Make sure your integrity is real. Check the reasons behind the reasons you are involved in church ministry, and challenge the purity of your motives.

ONE APPLICATION

1. What is the one personal application in reassessing your motives?

2. What is the one church application in examining its motives?

CHAPTER 7

REALIZE THE FEAR ELEMENT

God is our refuge and strength, a very present help in trouble. Therefore we will not fear though the earth gives way, though the mountains be moved into the heart of the sea, though its waters roar and foam, though the mountains tremble at its swelling. Selah.

—Psalm 46:1-3

The Challenges

→ *Fear is real for most Christians.*

→ *There are too many "What if's."*

→ *There is a real fear behind the fear.*

→ *What does faith over fear mean?*

The first and most natural feeling encountered as the news of the coronavirus hit our eyes and ears was *fear*. And no one was exempt, Christians and non-Christians alike, young and old, Eastern and Western nations, healthy and unhealthy, all fearing the worst.

It was real. We all felt it. It got to us without any warning and gripped us. It stirred us up and messed us up. It got us talking and got us searching. It got us worried and anxious. It freaked most people and even paralyzed some.

We began to fear not only the *virus,* we even began to fear other *humans.* It seemed like everyone was a potential threat and everyone was to be feared.

The fear was so real that it totally locked people up emotionally as well as physically. A few of my neighbors have not been out of their homes for a few weeks now, and here in Western Australia, we are not even under such tight measures.

I am not aware of any other event or situation in modern history to have brought such levels of fear worldwide.

This fear has closed up nations, states, cities, businesses, offices, factories, transportation, schools, event venues, sport stadiums, and even churches. No one was spared.

What are we learning? The church has to realize that we are living in one of the most *fear-driven* periods in history. It may not be so vivid as other calamities of the past, but the fear in society is very real right now. The church also needs to realize that most Christians, one way or another, are deeply affected by this fear. And this cannot be ignored.

Christianity generally shows a brave face to the world and its language is often entrenched in faith sayings of the Bible. This is wonderful to see and hear; however, I am not sure how real it is for those proclaiming them.

One of the sayings that developed recently, and I even held a sermon on this topic as did many other preachers, was "faith over fear." It sounds uplifting and awesome! But how real is it out there in the everyday trenches?

One of the best tests that the Lord prompted me to undertake during this COVID-19 period had to do with how I am handling the current fear crisis. He challenged me with this internal inquiry, "Why do you ask the 'What if' questions?"

What If?

Like me, you may have asked yourself many "What if" questions during this time. Including:

- What if I or someone in my family gets the virus?

- What if someone close to me dies?

- What if I die?

- What if I lose my job or business?

- What if I can't pay the mortgage?

- What if I run out of money?

- What if I can't travel?

- What if I can't visit friends and family…for a few years?

- What if I can't attend church for months?

- What if the church falls away?

- What if church people are not faithful in giving?

- What if my church has to close the building permanently?

The What if list could carry on for pages.

The Lord confronted me, asking me why I ask these what-if questions. What do they bring? Doubt. Anxiety. Worry.

The simple answer to His question was that I wanted in one way or another to have some sort of control over the situation, to prepare to sort out these scenarios if they were to occur.

And here lies the problem. It's twofold. One, I wanted to control, as if I could. This humbled me. God is sovereign, I am not. He reigns, not me. He controls, not me. He is Lord of all, not me.

Two, they are scenarios, not realities. Again, face down on my knees. They are made-up stories that will most likely never happen. They are only in my mind, created because of fear being allowed to govern my mind. God prompted me to do a reality check. And I am learning.

As such, I am detoxing from "What if" scenarios. There are enough real issues to deal with that need my attention. And for those that could spring up in the future, I will deal with them as they come along. Worrying about them will only steal my joy of my current reality and cloud my perspective for the future.

So what is the mindset and perspective God wants us to have? He said to replace the "What if?" with "Even if."

Even If

The anchor the Lord wants us to have through this pandemic and all other unsettling situations in our lives is that *He is God* and we can be confident in His protection and in His power—*even if* a worst case scenario becomes reality.

King David reassured us of God's provision throughout life's toughest challenges. In one of his most famous writings, Psalm 23, he says in verse 4, *"Even though I walk through the valley of the shadow of death, **I will fear no evil**, for you are with me...."*

When we have the attitude that no matter what happens in the future, *even if* we go through the deepest valleys of our human experience, near-death experiences, we can fear nothing because

God is with us. This assurance wipes away the uncertainty that led to the fear in the first place.

The sons of Korah began Psalm 46 with God's provision during a difficult period. They wrote:

> **God is our refuge and strength,** *a very **present help** in trouble.* *Therefore **we will not fear** though the earth gives way, though the mountains be moved into the heart of the sea, though its waters roar and foam, though the mountains tremble at its swelling. Selah* (Psalm 46:1-3).

Notice the key words, *refuge, strength* and *present help.* God is a place of *refuge* for us during this pandemic. God is our strength, meaning He is strong for us and in us in the current and every situation. And more so, He is our *present help.* This highlights how important it is to have the awareness of the proximity of God. God is so close to us, ever present in the middle of our crisis. This is the secret of our confidence. God is Emmanuel—God with us. This awareness brings our confident proclamation, "Therefore we will not fear!"

It is often quoted that the Bible has 366 "Fear not" statements, one for each day of the year, including a leap year. God does not want us to go one day without His secure affirmation. He knows that every day we will face a battle—to choose faith over fear. We need to awaken to this reality, to deeply absorb these words, and let them become real.

By reading a few Bible verses and meditating over them, we see how our faith is being built up. We know that faith comes by hearing, accepting, and embodying the Word of God in us. As you read these lines, your faith is being built up by God's Word cited and then briefly explained.

So, let me ask you this. Where are believers at this very moment? Where are they in their Christian walk? What is the vibe out there in the Christian community? Has the church taught them to overcome fear? To be people in the Word and of the Word of God? Can they walk through this valley? Will they make it? Are they afraid? Why are Christians afraid?

Are You Afraid?

"Why are you afraid..." is the very question Jesus asked His disciples when they encountered a storm. Here's the short story:

*And when he [Jesus] got into the boat, his disciples followed him. And behold, there arose a great storm on the sea, so that the boat was being swamped by the waves; but he was asleep. And they went and woke him, saying, "Save us, Lord; we are perishing." And he said to them, "**Why are you afraid**, O you of little faith?" Then he rose and rebuked the winds and the sea, and there was a great calm. And the men marveled, saying, "What sort of man is this, that even winds and sea obey him?" (Matthew 8:23-27)*

Jesus gets in the boat with them to go to the other side of the sea. He knows the storm is coming and chooses to take them through the storm. It's what He does. He told us that we will go through storms, suffering, and tribulation in life, and He will be there with us. He probably did this to teach them, and us, a lesson. Then He goes to sleep. They wake Him up and He calms the storm, not before rebuking them for their fear and lack of faith—notice how these go hand in hand.

Essentially, the challenge Jesus gave them was, "Why are you so afraid even though you have Me with you in the boat? You know I am the Son of God and you have seen many miracles. What is wrong with your faith? You are afraid because your faith is little. You haven't banked up enough faith in Me to even go through a storm with Me in your boat."

Yes, COVID-19 is a fearsome storm. Yes, lives are in danger. Yes, the danger is real. Yes, the sea is stormy. Yes, the boat is rocking. Yes, the waves are coming in. But our boat is different from all other boats out there on the worldwide sea. In our boat rests Jesus! Yes, in the middle of the storm, He rests. His identity is not affected by the storm. His peace is not stolen by the storm. And He promised us that very same rest and peace for troubled times.

Jesus calmed the storm. He will calm this storm, too. We worship a storm-calming God. Storms obey Him. Winds obey Him. Seas obey Him. Nature obeys Him. Coronavirus obeys Him.

How well have we presented Christ to others? How real is God's sovereignty in us? How strong is our faith? Sharing it with others is their hope—their rest and peace. Our challenge in this time is to build faith in people. Whether through social media, phone calls, or home visits, we are called to rally them on into faith.

Fear will not just dissipate. Fear is a real emotion that can freeze people. We need to help people rise above the fear by building their faith. Little faith is not good enough. Jesus said that little faith is characterized by being equal to being afraid. Only strong faith overcomes the fear element.

We have been given a measure of faith (Romans 12:3), and it is our responsibility to grow that faith. Pastors may have failed to prepare the people not just for the coronavirus but for anything that life may bring. The current situation has highlighted how unprepared people are and how we have work to do. And we need to go even deeper.

The Fear Behind the Fear

What then is the real fear out there? Is it the fear of contracting the coronavirus? Is it the fear of being sick? Is it the fear of losing wealth? Or is there something deeper beneath this coronavirus fear?

I believe that the real fear behind the fear is the all-consuming fear—*the fear of dying.* This is the fear that not many talk about, yet it's the deep root of all our fears.

Most people are afraid of death. Even many Christians are afraid of death. Everyone knows this. Governments know this. The media knows this. The business world knows this. And they play with this fact in people's minds. If you watch the daily news or scroll through social media, you are swamped with fear-triggering stories of gloom and doom. And that is how the masses are controlled.

This is pretty bad news for most people, except for us Christians. This is where we can shine. This is where we can bring hope. This is where we have an opportunity to talk about life beyond death.

We have renewed minds. We have a renewed perspective. We see life as God sees it, and we have hope beyond this life.

Let me remind of you this powerful reassurance found in Hebrews 2:14-15:

> *Since therefore the children share in flesh and blood, he himself likewise partook of the same things, that through death he might destroy the one who has the power of death, that is, the devil, and deliver all those who through fear of death were subject to lifelong slavery.*

Let's briefly break down this passage:

- We are God's children.

- We took part in all that He has done for us.

- Through Jesus' death He destroyed the devil, who has power of death.

- Through His death, Jesus delivered those who were enslaved by the fear of death.

Jesus destroyed both the *fear of dying* and *death* itself on the cross. Because we are one with Him in His death, we are also one with Him in His resurrection. Romans 6:5 reaffirms this, *"For if we have been united with him in a death like his, we shall certainly be united with him in a resurrection like his."*

What is astounding is that the New Testament refers to those who have died as having *fallen asleep.* Even the word "cemetery" comes from the Greek term *koimetorion,* which means sleeping place. When someone falls asleep, there is an expectation to wake up.

The apostle Paul described this nicely in 1 Thessalonians 4:13-14 (NIV):

> *Brothers and sisters, we do not want you to be uninformed about **those who sleep in death**, so that you do not grieve like the rest of mankind, who have no hope. For we believe that Jesus died and rose again, and so **we believe that God will bring with Jesus those who have fallen asleep in him.***

As children of God we must encourage each other to look beyond this life. We were warned by the apostle Paul that, *"If in Christ we have hope in this life only, we are of all people most to be pitied"* (1 Corinthians 15:19).

Life takes full meaning when we truly embrace *the resurrection.* That is our most glorious chapter, not this life. Colossians 3:4 brings this message home, *"When Christ who is your life appears, then you also will appear with him in glory."* And this takes us back to faith, a faith that rises above any fear.

Faith Over Fear

The question you and people you meet may be challenged with right now is, "Why am I still experiencing fear even though I believe I have faith?"

Fear is an emotion that everyone experiences every time you feel threatened. It is one of the most powerful human emotions, and it is God-given. It protects us. It is to be used to fear God.

Feeling fear is not a sin. Giving in to fear is. Obeying fear is. Fear must drive us to faith. We have a choice to make, to take the emotion and make it a reality, or to choose faith in God over that emotion.

The question then is, "What are we doing when we are afraid?" To whom do we turn? We go to our object of faith—to God, our solid rock. When God told Joshua to be strong and courageous, He also told him why he is able to be exactly that—because the Lord God was with him wherever he went (Joshua 1:9).

We can conform to the fear patterns of the world or we can be people of faith who choose to be strong and courageous in the middle of the coronavirus pandemic.

Our role as people of faith in this season is to help our family, friends, neighbors, and community to rise above their fear and increase their faith in God every day. I cannot emphasize this, every day, enough.

We also need to look around and awaken to the reality that most people are afraid. We have the antidote for their fear—Jesus, the Savior of the world. We can bring hope to those around us by sharing His ever-faithful presence. This is an opportunity we cannot miss.

ONE APPLICATION

1. What is the one thing you lack when it comes to dealing with fear?
2. What is the one thing your church is lacking in dealing with fear?

CHAPTER 8

RESTORE THE WHOLE PERSON

When Jesus saw him lying there and knew that he had already been there a long time, he said to him, "Do you want to be healed?"

—John 5:6

The Challenges

→ *The church should be a place of holistic restoration.*

→ *The church is full of people emotionally, mentally, and physically unwell.*

→ *The church has followed patterns of the world in restoration.*

→ *Post pandemic, the church needs a holistic restoration and sanctification strategy.*

Three years ago I received a call from a young Christian mother needing some emotional intelligence coaching. Among the first questions I asked her was to tell me what she really wanted, what was her desired outcome. She found it difficult to express exactly what she wanted, so I asked her to do a Yes/No exercise with me.

The exercise was to identify what she was saying "yes" to; and for each yes there had to be at least three "no" things in order to achieve the desired result. She began with a yes outcome and then without giving too much thought, she had to tell me what she was saying no to, to achieve that goal. The no list became very long, quickly. As she was expanding the list and going through the exercise, she realized that for every yes to be achieved, there were lots of nos that she had to embrace. And that became uneasy. She began to realize where she was in her emotional state. It was an awakening. She had never been this aware of her reality. And that frightened her.

She then said, "I don't want to do this anymore."

I asked why.

She said, "Because it makes me aware of my issues and I don't want to deal with them."

Then I simply asked her, "Do you want to be made well?"

She said, "I do, but I don't. I would rather not."

And she didn't.

This is not uncommon. Some people want to be well, and others prefer to remain as they are. They avoid the responsibility that comes with being healthy, so they prefer to maintain a needy or victim mentality.

Our churches are full of people who are *unwell*. It's a sad reality. A few are restored while most remain the same. Many churches have learned to live and coexist with such people and make every effort not to unsettle them too much, keeping them under manageable control.

The coronavirus pandemic is awakening us to a new reality. Church people are affected mentally and emotionally by the lockdown, by the prospect of losing their jobs and businesses, and they are in real need of support.

Just yesterday, May 13, 2020, the Australian government created a new deputy chief medical position amid coronavirus mental health fears. They are forecasting major mental health issues ahead, related to the distress and overwhelming consequences of the coronavirus.

The church will also be expecting an influx of people who, being deeply affected by the isolation and side effects of the virus, will look for a place where they can be nurtured, loved, and restored.

Depending where you are in the world, some people who will come through the church door might have already suffered directly from COVID, either by having contracted it and lived through it, or having lost someone dear. The church has to be aware of this need and rise up to it. Jesus touched well on this.

Jesus' Way of Full Restoration

While walking through the streets of Jerusalem on a Sabbath for one of the Jewish festivals, Jesus stopped by the pool of Bethesda, a place full of broken people in need of healing. They were there because occasionally an angel came down to stir up the waters, and whoever jumped in first was cured (John 5:2-9).

A man who had been an invalid for thirty-eight years was waiting for someone to assist him into the water when the stir occurred. Every time he wanted to jump in, someone else would go in before him and be restored. He missed out every time as he depended on someone else's help, and he had no one.

Jesus comes into the scene and sees him. He knew of the man's thirty-eight years suffering. So, Jesus asks him, *"Do you want to be healed?"* (John 5:6). The question seems rather odd. It is quite surprising. Shouldn't Jesus just pick up the man, carry him to the pool, wait for the stir, and lower him in? Simpler yet, He could just heal him. Why ask the man this question? If someone is hungry, you give him food; if someone is thirsty, you give him water. You don't generally ask if he is hungry or thirsty.

The question is profound and needs deeper inquiry. Jesus is asking a lot more in this question. What is Jesus really asking of the man?

1. Jesus is asking the man what he wants, what does he desire. Jesus' question reveals something important about God and about us. God invites us to question and explore our *desires*. What do we really want and why do we want it? Do we really want to be healed?

Some part of me wants to continue the role of innocent victim, to blame others for offending or wounding me, or for keeping me stuck. Some parts of me like to complain and to look for excuses, to look how my parents, my spouse, or my children have let me down, and I deserve better as this is not my fault. I could have been well, but because of what happened I am stuck on the side of the pool, with healing so close, but never quite making the move.

It is an honest self-examination that goes deep into our motives and our desires until we find the bedrock of what we really want. And as we dig deep and sift through all our lesser wants, we may discover that we want to be fully alive, *holistically well.*

2. Jesus is asking the man if he wants whole restoration. The question in another Bible translation is, "Do you want to be made *whole?*" His paralysis affected all areas of his life, not just his physical body. Healing the body is important, but only one part of the process. Jesus knew this man needed to be restored *completely.* Jesus came to bring whole restoration. He wants to wholly restore not only the body, but the soul as well—our mind, will and emotions.

While it would have been easier to simply heal the man and keep on walking, Jesus chose to ask the man for a response and demand an action. Jesus said to him, *"Get up, take up your bed, and walk"* (John 5:8). The instructions were clear. They demanded a response. The lame man could have chosen not to follow the instructions and remain in his crippled condition—or get up, pick up his mat, and experience full restoration. We know what he did: *"And at once the man was healed, and he took up his bed and walked."* Amazing.

Many ministries and churches, in their efforts to help the broken and oppressed, shift the levels of dependence from one addiction to another, almost encouraging dependence on ongoing assistance, handouts, and institutional care or medication. Christ-centered wholeness is a result of experiencing freedom from any dependency and the ability to journey with the Lord as the Source of wholeness.

It begins with God's intention of full restoration of all things to His image, and it has to be centered on the transformational power of Jesus Christ, through whom all things are restored. The church has to realize that unless it focuses on the person of Christ for full restoration, all other well-intended ministries will only scratch the surface.

Jesus has the unique ability to restore all areas of our lives. When we are broken and unwell, we are not reflecting His image in us. He wants to fully restore us, to make all things whole again.

3. Jesus is asking the man if he wants to be responsible for his life. Do you want to move forward in your life? Do you want to rise up spiritually? Do you want to make progress emotionally? Do you want a renewed way of thinking? Do you want to willfully surrender to the lordship of Jesus?

The challenge churches are facing today is that many people do not want to be healed. They do not want to receive divine healing and divine help with their problems. They do not want to be helped out of their weakness. They are comfortable with their weakness and helplessness. Some crave attention through their helplessness. And they reject assuming responsibility for their own lives.

The crippled man wanted to be healed, but he couldn't jump into the water. He tried everything he knew and all that he could, but lacked the ability. He gave up. He saw no way, from a human point of view. So he resigned himself to sitting there beside the pool.

The way the Lord heals him is remarkable: *"Get up, take up your bed, and walk"* (John 5:8).

First, Jesus asks the man to do the impossible—rise. To get up required *faith!* It was a word of *action.* All of the sudden the man believed he could stand, and he did.

Then, second, Jesus removes all possibility of a relapse and tells the man to take up his bed—roll it up, pack it up, you're done with this. You are not coming back here tomorrow. Get rid of your bed. You will not relapse into your old crippling state. There is no provision for you to go back on the miracle that the Lord has made in your life. Burn your bridges.

And third, Jesus expects a continued success—walk. Do not expect to be carried. You walk now. It is time to be responsible for your life, to walk in the new identity!

Like this man, Jesus gave you the power to rise, to let go of your infirmity, and He will give you the power to walk every day, to keep on going. You are no longer looking at passersby to help you—you have your eyes on Jesus. His power has worked in you and is working in you every day. Christ in you is your everyday hope!

Where does Jesus find the man shortly after? The man had gone into the temple because the Law required a thanksgiving offering (John 5:13-14). Look now at the way Jesus speaks to him and the order of the summary of what happened to him in the healing.

> *Now the man who had been healed did not know who it was, for Jesus had withdrawn, as there was a crowd in the place. Afterward Jesus found him in the temple and said to him, "See, you are well! Sin no more, that nothing worse may happen to you"* (John 5:13-14).

Instead of saying to him directly, "Sin no more," Jesus began with, "See, you are well!" In other words, you have been made whole. What you experienced is not just physical healing, you have also been spiritually healed. Your sins were forgiven, you have been washed and cleansed, and you are now a new man. Everything is renewed in you and made whole—your physical body, your soul, and your spirit. Once you are aware of this total renewal, of this amazing gift of God without any merit on your part, Jesus says, "Sin no more."

The final verse in this story gives us hope for our times. Jesus finishes saying, *"My Father is working until now, and I am working"* (John 5:17). This is one of the most profound statements in the Gospel of John. The secret of meaning in anyone's life is to discover what God is doing and become His instrument in that chapter of history.

Jesus reminds us that God is working throughout history, even today during the coronavirus pandemic. And Jesus engages to work with God in His restoration of humanity. The church is called today to look at what the Father is doing and to engage exactly in that. God is at work and the church should be at work. God restores the whole person and we should be the instruments of that full restoration.

If healing is important to Christianity, it has to be restored to its rightful place in the church's life. And this healing has to be holistic.

Complete Restoration and Sanctification

The apostle Paul understood the idea of complete restoration. He also understood that we needed compete sanctification—spirit, soul, and body—not just spiritual sanctification. But what is even more amazing about the way Paul made sense of it all is the order, the alignment, of these three.

Read what Paul writes to the believers in Thessalonica: *Now may the **God of peace** himself **sanctify you completely**, and may your whole spirit and soul and body be kept blameless at the coming of our Lord Jesus Christ* (1 Thessalonians 5:23).

God Himself is the God of peace, and He is the One who does the complete work of sanctification in us. He starts with our spirit, who connects to God's Holy Spirit. Order is critical here.

Everything is spiritual first! All is spiritual! I cannot emphasize this enough for every believer. And because everything is spiritual, deal with this first in everything.

The world has flipped the flow. And the church has slowly slipped into this pattern. It's all about the body, then the soul, and hardly anytime about the spirit. The first focus of most people is the body, either the look or the health and vitality of their body. It's most likely because that is what we see first. But being too preoccupied with the body as our priority is not godly.

In fact, we will never achieve complete restoration if we start with the body. The body may give us the signals, but the correct order is to deal with everything in the spirit, first.

Once most people work on their body restoration, they begin to think about their mind. And this is an important work that takes a great deal of time. They try to change their thinking, their mindset, their perspective, their thought patterns. They also work on their will, on discipline, on clarity, on decision making, and this is absolutely needed.

In the past twenty years and more so in recent times, there's been a huge awareness of the need for emotional intelligence. This is the space I work in in my coaching practice. It's critical to be aware of our emotions and learn how to manage them.

But all of these take us only so far, and even getting this far is laborious work most people will not undertake.

Many people accomplish much in life, yet still feel a spiritual vacuum. This void has always been there and will always be there. Some sense it early in their spiritual journey, others chase after the wind all their lives realizing they're not getting anywhere. By the time they look for spiritual meaning and self-transcendence, they have been messed up with New Age worldviews that take them into a dark spiritual place.

Imagine now if we, the church, grabbed hold of this powerful spiritual truth. Complete restoration has a divine order—spirit, soul, and body.

Complete restoration is not really complete without complete sanctification. That's why the apostle Paul emphasized sanctification. It is critical. And dealing with the spirit first, aligns the soul and the body. Sanctifying the spirit ripples down in sanctifying the soul—mind, will, and emotions—and finally, the body.

As God's holy people, the church, please, please understand me. This pandemic is giving us the most amazing opportunity for restoration of so many people we know. Take them to the Lord for spiritual restoration and sanctification first. *Then,* talk about their mind, will, and emotions. And by then, the body's restoration and sanctification will become a by-product of what has already happened in the spirit and in the soul—in that order.

Focus on the spirit! Spirit first. Soul next. Body last.

The body cannot be kept blameless until Jesus returns in any other way. Look at how many Christians all around you are struggling. Our churches are full of them. They struggle in their bodies. They struggle in their minds in their decision making and with their emotions.

We've been okay with this for far too long! If the church is not spiritual, who out there is? If Christians don't bring spiritual meaning and restoration, who will? If not you and me, who?

The goal of this chapter is to awaken the church to this spiritual reality. The need for full restoration has never been so evident as it is now. Post pandemic, this could be our biggest challenge. It could be our most fruitful era of the church.

The next chapter of church life, be it in full gatherings or in homes for a while, must be a chapter when the church engages in full restoration of people, both existing members and newcomers. It is God's divine order.

And in fact, you know what? God does this. We just need to guide people into engaging with God. Help them see and prioritize God's full restoration and sanctification.

ONE APPLICATION

1. What is the one lesson you will apply from this chapter for yourself?

2. What is the one lesson your church will apply?

CHAPTER 9

REFRESH YOUR PERSPECTIVE

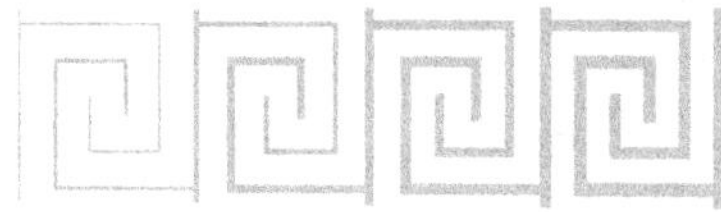

The eye is the lamp of the body. So, if your eye is healthy,
your whole body will be full of light.

—Matthew 6:22

The Challenges

→ *The church is confronted with a worldly worldview toward the coronavirus pandemic characterized by fear and uncertainty.*

→ *The outlook is dim for most people, and there is an anxious wait for the future.*

→ *Perspective is not something the church taught as a priority.*

→ *The church has to rise above the current situation and bring a heavenly perspective full of hope and certainty.*

My brother-in-law said something profound to me the other day as we were talking about the current pandemic and the lockdown that came with it. He said, "You know, Natanael, people keep saying that we're in the same boat with the current situation.

I thought about it and I don't believe we're in the same boat. We are in the same *storm,* but not in the same *boat.*"

What Caleb was talking about was *perspective.* Each person has a different perspective on the current crisis; and even though many of these tend to seem the same, every person has to deal *personally* with his or her daily changing views.

The lenses we see through determine our attitude, thinking, and behavior toward this challenging period of history. Our upbringing, conditioning, and worldview also play major roles. What we watch, who we listen to, and more so where we allow our mind to wander, will unconsciously shape our perspective just as much.

What are we learning as a church in this season? We are learning that we are to help people refresh their perspective. We need to remind them of God's hand and provision in history. We are called to lift them to a higher perspective and lead them into the heavenly worldview—or better yet, a God-view. We have the responsibility to care for them with a healthy outlook. This refreshing is not just for now, it is from now on.

A Historical Perspective

The Lord invites us to open our eyes and see Him at work in the historical accounts of the Bible to get a healthy historical perspective on His providence.

The story of Jehoshaphat in 2 Chronicles 20 brings this into our frame of reference. As the king of Judah, he encountered a major crisis when a massive army came to war against him. They had no chance against this great army, so he assembled the people and began to pray:

"O Lord, God of our fathers, are you not God in heaven? You rule over all the kingdoms of the nations. In your hand

are power and might, so that none is able to withstand you. Did you not, our God, drive out the inhabitants of this land before your people Israel, and give it forever to the descendants of Abraham your friend? And they have lived in it and have built for you in it a sanctuary for your name, saying, 'If disaster comes upon us, the sword, judgment, or pestilence, or famine, we will stand before this house and before you—for your name is in this house—and cry out to you in our affliction, and you will hear and save.' And now behold, the men of Ammon and Moab and Mount Seir, whom you would not let Israel invade when they came from the land of Egypt, and whom they avoided and did not destroy—behold, they reward us by coming to drive us out of your possession, which you have given us to inherit. O our God, will you not execute judgment on them? For we are powerless against this great horde that is coming against us. We do not know what to do, but our eyes are on you" (2 Chronicles 20:6-12).

It's fascinating to break down this Scripture passage and see how many characteristics of King Jehoshaphat's dependence on God he listed in such a short prayer.

1. Who God is:

- Lord
- God of our fathers
- God in heaven
- Ruler over all kingdoms and nations
- In Your hands are power and might
- None is able to withstand You
- Abraham's friend
- Our God
- You execute judgment

2. What God has promised:
- Your name to be in this house
- You will hear and save
- This land is our inheritance from you

3. What God has done:
- You drove out others before, to give us this land
- You gave this land to us

4. What we will do:
- We will keep our eyes on You

Jehoshaphat needed to exhibit leadership to the people of Judah through a life-threatening crisis. He reminded them of who God was, what He had promised, what He had done, and how dependent they were on Him. The historical evidence of God's character, promises, and His actions lifted the king to a higher perspective, and he took the people with him into this perspective.

The church today has a responsibility to refresh people's minds of the historical acts of God throughout recent and past history. These historical records serve us with faith-building pillars that sustain us with a godly perspective.

A Higher Perspective

In the Introduction of this book I mentioned briefly Joseph's perspective on his life challenges. His brothers sold him into Egyptian slavery and then because he refused to sleep with his boss's wife, he ended up for many years in prison.

Most people would have accumulated bitterness, resentment, and hatred. Rather, Joseph raised his perspective above all the pain and unfair imprisonment to gain a godly outlook. We don't really know whether he had this perspective in the middle of the crisis or soon after. But the fact that he came out of it with such drive and disposition to help Pharaoh and the affairs of Egypt to prepare for the famine to come, demonstrates that Joseph had a higher perspective. Pharaoh's confession that God's Spirit abides in Joseph (Genesis 41:38) also reveals that even as he came out of prison, Joseph had maintained a heavenly outlook.

The climax of Joseph's higher perspective is seen when he addresses his brothers: *"As for you, you meant evil against me, but **God meant it for good**, to bring it about that **many people should be kept alive**, as they are today"* (Genesis 50:20).

I am sure that many evil people were excited to see the churches close their doors. I also know that many Christians have been deeply affected by the closures. But if we are to rise to a higher perspective, we know that God is meaning this *for good*. And that brings a comforting outlook.

There is another aspect to this verse in Genesis 50 that we are tempted to neglect but seems very appropriate in our current scene. Joseph saw that the reason God meant it for good was to keep people alive.

We are asked to stay in isolation to protect lives. God is keeping people alive through this lockdown. What if this is His way of working it out for us, to keep us alive? What if through this He is also working to bring His church into being *more alive?* His ways are better than ours and by drawing close to them, we will begin to see them (Isaiah 55:8).

A Healthy Perspective

Jesus spoke about having a healthy perspective, especially when it comes to worrying. Worry is the result of wrong outlook.

The anxiety of what the future will bring has to do with the way we look at each situation. Are we afraid? Are we fatalist? Are we hopeless? These worries only take us in a downward spiral into destruction.

Jesus invites us to come up higher. He said, *"The eye is the lamp of the body. So, if your eye is healthy, your whole body will be full of light"* (Matthew 6:22). Your perspective is the doorway to your body. If you have a healthy perspective, your whole body will be healthy—full of light. If you have an unhealthy perspective, your whole body will be unhealthy—full of darkness.

Where does the church come in? The church has every reason to rise above the current situation and lead its people into a higher perspective. It cannot be dragged down in dismay and despair. Throughout history it has had challenges and threats. Every generation had to deal with some sort of crisis, whether it was internal or external. My parents had to deal with persecution in communist Romania, and my grandparents suffered through two world wars and the Spanish flu pandemic. Today's challenges are not that far off.

I know we read Romans 8:28 quite often to encourage one another, and it's great that we do. But do we truly believe it or has it become a Christian cliché verse?

And we know that for those who love God all things work together for good, for those who are called according to his purpose (Romans 8:28).

This verse gives us vital ammunition when it comes to perspective. Let's dig deep.

1. **We know.** This is not something we just believe or hope for, something that may or may not happen. We are talking about conviction here, knowledge and certainty. We know that God is in all things. We know that He can and will sort it out. We have absolute assurance and we know of that assurance.

2. ***For those who love God.*** We are not like the rest of the world, afraid and disoriented. We have a relationship with God and we love God. For us things sit differently. There is a grace for people who know and love God. He is our heavenly Father who cares and provides for us. You are part of His family. You have that identity.

3. ***All things work together for good.*** Yes, *all* things. Everything. Nothing is accidental. God does not make mistakes. God is not taken by surprise. All things are under His control. And all things will work together for His good. In one Bible translation it says that He *causes* all things to work together for good. Generally we see this in retrospect. We have seen how every situation in our lives has done something amazingly good in us. Yes, even through this pandemic God is working things for good.

4. ***For those who are called according to His purpose.*** That is us. That is His church, His body on earth. We are called according to His purposes. God is for us! God is for you and me. He causes everything to work together for good for His purposes, and we are the people called to be part of those purposes. We have a role to play as beneficiaries of His goodness, so long as we remain in His plans and purposes.

A Personal Perspective Encounter

Some years ago, in my youth, I was facing a crossroad in life, and I had to make a decision. So, I decided to ask the Lord for guidance. I said, "God, please guide me in the direction I should take. Should I go left, right, or turn back?" I prayed and waited on the Lord. As I was waiting, He replied in my thought, "It doesn't matter."

I was confused. "Lord, what do You mean it doesn't matter? Here I am asking You for direction and You're telling me it doesn't matter? I normally don't even ask You and I do as I will. But now when I'm asking You to guide me, You're telling me it doesn't matter? Please Lord, left, right, forward, or backward?"

The response was the same, "Natanael, it does not matter."

I became a little irritated by His reply. I asked, "What do You mean it doesn't matter? God, I truly want to do Your will. I want to have a clear direction in this decision and You are telling me that it doesn't matter. What am I to make of this? I don't get it. I want to listen to You. I am here to obey You. Please just tell me what path to take, and whether I like it or not, I will do it according to Your guidance. Please tell me which way I should go!"

Then the gentle voice of the Lord came and said, "Natanael, come up higher."

In a vision, the Lord took me above the intersection. Yes, I could see the crossroad, and the four directions that were available. Then the Lord stretched His hand over the intersection and began to move the intersection to the left and to the right.

He said, "Natanael, I am God! I can move the whole intersection in My favor. I am God over every intersection and over the whole world and universe. Do not think of Me as a road sign, as a traffic light or as a GPS. I am not here just to guide you at a crossroad in life. I am here to be your God! I am here to care for you not just in this situation, but as a loving Father, in every moment of your life. Know that I am God. I am God over the intersection and I can adjust and move the whole intersection in the direction I desire, so it does not matter which way you choose to go. What matters is to make Me Lord over your life, over every decision and over every situation."

I repented. I wept. I realized that I was reducing God to my perspective while He was inviting me into His. My eyes—my perspective—were not healthy until I was taken into a higher perspective.

The church is invited into a godly perspective. If we don't offer that to the anxious world around us, who will? We have to rise above the current pandemic and bring a healthy, divine outlook, an outlook full of hope and full of God.

The church has an amazing opportunity to testify to the world who God is by the way it responds to this crisis, by the perspective it offers. It saddens me to see the social media flooded with videos of doom times, videos produced and uploaded by Christian leaders. We cannot go on the path of dissolution and despair. It is a deception. Our eyes must be healthy! When our eyes are healthy, the whole church body is healthy. The church is called to rise above this and be a light on a hill, to bring hope, godly direction, and godly perspective. Let's do that!

ONE APPLICATION

1. What is the one shift this chapter brings into your personal life?

2. What is the one shift your church will make from this chapter?

CHAPTER 10

REDISCOVER DISCIPLESHIP

And he said to all, "If anyone would come after me, let him deny himself and take up his cross daily and follow me."

—Luke 9:23

The Challenges

→ *Discipleship in church is highly sought but poorly taught.*

→ *Many pastors never became true disciples themselves.*

→ *The coronavirus exposed discipleship as the church's biggest challenge.*

→ *Discipleship needs a fresh inquiry at every level of the church.*

My very first subject in Bible college was Discipleship. When I enrolled I thought, *Is this a real subject?* I understood a bit about the breakdown of the topics to be studied in a Bible school such as doctrines, homiletics, hermeneutics, Bible book studies, even leadership, but discipleship? Where does that fit in?

This was in the year 2000, not that long ago. What was even more strange was the fact that no one in the class knew what to expect.

This class was taught in two parts for the whole year, two semesters. I wondered, *What will they teach us about discipleship? Our churches hardly ever spoke about this, except as the Lord's teaching, most likely for His era when He needed someone to take on His message to the world.*

Then Dr. Bob Chapman—who later became my spiritual mentor and more so, my spiritual father—stepped into the scene. It was his class, and from the very first word he challenged us beyond measure. He said, "In this life it is you and Jesus alone." We didn't agree. He was right though. He said, "True Christianity is a full commitment to the Lord Jesus Christ." We agreed with this in principle, but definitely not in practice. "Nothing less than complete surrender is fit enough for following Christ," he would say. Yes, preach it brother, then forget it.

And through every sentence, at every page turn, through every example and illustration, we were on the edge of our seats, challenged to the core. He turned us inside out and exposed the very deep desires of our hearts. It was frightening to see what was hidden behind the layers of our inner being. Gently, but firmly, he removed them one by one. Eventually some left his class as it became too confronting. Others, like me, allowed the stir, the discomfort, the renewal, the pain of dealing with my carnality, and went deep, repenting and weeping while discovering the path of discipleship.

The impact of Dr. Bob Chapman's introduction to discipleship was life transforming for me. I became, what he later told me, his best student. He equipped many people in discipleship, and a small percentage took on his teaching in full measure. I was one of them. The effect was so profound it became the topic of my first book, *Forty Years and Forty Days,* for which Dr. Chapman wrote the Foreword. I wrote the book in forty days from my fortieth birthday, a chapter a day, at 4 a.m. during forty days of fasting and prayer.

The book has forty spiritual lessons that impacted my life to the age of forty, mostly immersed in my discipleship journey. Every morning

I emailed to Dr. Chapman the chapter I wrote, and he would run through it and lightly edit it without distorting the revelation. He was celebrating my journey while also keeping me accountable. It was a marathon forty days in which he held my hand and kept my focus on Jesus. I am still in deep awe just thinking and writing about this amazing life journey.

I don't know your journey in discipleship, but I am absolutely sure that if you have turned to Christ and have begun a genuine walk with the Lord, this has already started. Where you are on this journey is dependent on the surrender you have made so far. My invitation in this chapter is to rediscover discipleship for yourself, before you even let your mind begin to think on how to bring it to people in your family or church.

Why is this important? This is important because the current situation with the coronavirus has exposed us at the individual level, but more so at the church level that we don't do discipleship well. Church members have difficulty dealing with the lockdown that brought loss of jobs, church closures, and a cloud of fear worldwide.

What this situation has uncovered for us is that folks in churches are not strong enough to stand on their own as followers of Christ. Many are immature. A large number are inconsistent. Most cannot walk the spiritual walk on their own on a daily basis. Some are falling by the wayside.

Why is this? They are *church* dependent. They are *pastor* dependent. They depend on the church for their spiritual nutrition, spiritual compass, spiritual teaching, spiritual fellowship, even for Bible study, prayer, and worship.

Why? Pastors and church leadership made them that way. We are guilty just as much as they are.

Allow me please to unpack, in a raw and simple way, discipleship. Please open your heart to rediscover this for yourself and engage in this at a personal level, then pray it will ripple into your wider circles. Let it begin with you, please.

Why am I so determined to work with you in this chapter? It is because this is *your church's biggest challenge.* If you can get this sorted with priority, all else will align in your church. It is one of the most important keys missing in Christendom right now. And this is your opportunity to reclaim discipleship for yourself and for others. If you get this right, your legacy will outlive you for generations to come! So let's begin.

Jesus *Invites* You to Be His Disciple

The invitation to discipleship is made by Jesus Himself. When He invited the first men who later became His disciples, Jesus invited them to follow Him. Jesus did not invite them to a religion, not even to Christianity as such. He invited them into a process of becoming like Him.

Let's recall the high invitation Jesus made as this is vital.

While walking by the Sea of Galilee, he saw two brothers, Simon (who is called Peter) and Andrew his brother, casting a net into the sea, for they were fishermen. And he said to them, "Follow me, and I will make you fishers of men." Immediately they left their nets and followed him. And going on from there he saw two other brothers, James the son of Zebedee and John his brother, in the boat with Zebedee their father, mending their nets, and he called them. Immediately they left the boat and their father and followed him (Matthew 4:18-22).

Jesus, recognized as a teacher, a rabbi, invites these men to follow Him. The greatest honor anyone could have in Israel was to be a rabbi.

They were highly sought people and every mother's dream was for her boy to one day become a rabbi.

The boys would memorize the Torah; and at the age of 13 when they celebrated bar mitzvah, they would recite verses from it. Through this ritualistic passage the boy became a man who could now lead the family into prayer. From this age he would learn the rest of the Old Testament and memorize it, hoping one of the rabbis would invite him to become his apprentice, or disciple. The highest honor was to be invited into discipleship.

It's critical to understand this if we are to grasp why the men left their businesses (nets), even their fathers, and followed Jesus. It was the greatest invitation they could receive! So they took it. It was the chance of their lifetime, and they were not going to let it pass by. They captured the moment and went for it without looking back.

I plead with readers who are pastors, ministers, church leaders, and fathers. Accept the invitation to follow Jesus with all of your heart for yourself first. Follow Him out of your love for Him. Make Him the greatest priority in your life, truly so, with love and passion. Present Jesus as worth following by demonstrating it. Then extend the invitation to others.

When Christians look at the invitation to discipleship made by Jesus, most look down on it as being sacrificial and unattractive. They don't see the honor and amazing call to become like the Master. We have not made it attractive. We have not made it highly invitational. We have not modeled it ourselves with passion.

The call to discipleship Jesus made to the men was to follow Him. He did not call them to a concept, teaching, movement, or even a religion. He called them to make them like Him. They were to become like Him! The invitation is into a process for His purposes. His purposes are always attractive, but the process is not. The process is very confronting.

Also, our tendency is to call people to our church, to our program, to our course, and to our following. We want people to become *our* disciples. This is wrong!

Jesus made disciples of *Himself*. They were His disciples. What happens next is critical for us to understand. The first generation of disciples also made disciples, but they did not make disciples of themselves. They made disciples of their Master. They made *disciples of Jesus!* This is where we often fail in our disciple making. We want to make disciples of ourselves.

Let me make a note here, before I expand on this. I believe we should be worth following, absolutely. I believe we are responsible for our practical testimony. I believe we should definitely model a Christ-like life. I strongly believe we should say and do as the apostle Paul said, *"Be imitators of me, as I am of Christ"* (1 Corinthians 11:1).

But, ultimately, we have to make disciples of Jesus Christ. Please hear me out. Stop making disciples of your church, your movement, your doctrine, your ways, your charisma, your talent, or anything of yours, please! Let's rediscover what it means to make disciples of Jesus.

That's why so many of our church members are disillusioned right now with the coronavirus situation. They are not true disciples of Jesus. They may be great followers of the church, of the culture, movement, and maybe even great followers of the pastor. But are they disciples of Jesus?

What happens if the pastor isn't there? What if the pastor moves away, gets sick, or falls into sin (God forbid), or dies? What if the church remains shut for the next six or even twelve months? Who is with church members in the middle of the night when they are sick? Who will look after them when they battle personal issues with no one around?

We are to make disciples of Jesus. Extend His high invitation into a true discipleship process. Disciple people into Jesus. Please, please make disciples of Jesus!

Jesus *Challenges* You to Be His Disciple

I stated that Jesus' call to discipleship was highly invitational. Well, it is just as much, highly challenging. Jesus is the Master at keeping these two in a healthy tension—the invitation and the challenge aspect of discipleship.

Here are the terms. Please accept them for yourself before you consider teaching them. Rediscover their personal application for yourself, then challenge others to model their lives according to these.

1. **A *love* above all others.**

    If anyone comes to me and does not hate his own father and mother and wife and children and brothers and sisters, yes, and even his own life, he cannot be my disciple (Luke 14:26).

The first term of discipleship is *love.* Our love for Christ must be so much above all others that they seem like hatred compared to the love for Him. The greatest challenge for us is not the hating of loved ones, it is hating our own life. Unless we are ready to lay down our lives for Him, we will never be His true disciples.

The love challenge is massive and it reveals who we truly are. The coronavirus situation has exposed our *loves.* This is applicable to all believers. Our love for Jesus may not be above all other loves, and that's why the present situation unsettles us. If we had given it all, forsaken it all, and have truly depended on Jesus, then one obstacle, regardless of size, be it coronavirus, should not unbalance us.

It affects us because our loves are not in order. When our love for God is above all other loves, then He aligns all other loves in our life.

2.   A true *denial* of self.

> *And he said to all, "If anyone would come after me, let him deny himself and take up his cross daily and follow me"* (Luke 9:23).

The denial of self is often misunderstood in Christendom. It is different and much deeper than self-denial. Self-denial means to give up something your self desires—food, drinks, hobby, etc.

Denial of self means to totally surrender your self (ego) to Jesus. It means to give up lordship and authority of your life to Jesus. It simply means to die to self. Only then will you truly live the life He came to give you. He revealed this secret, too.

> *For whoever would save his life will lose it, but whoever loses his life for my sake will save it* (Luke 9:24).

This statement is found in all of the four Gospels, even repeatedly (Matthew 10:30; 16:25; Mark 8:35; Luke 9:24; Luke 17:33; and John 12:25). Why? It is because it lays a genuine foundation of the new life in Christ.

Life only has real meaning when it is lived in the resurrection of Christ in the believer's life. Nobody can be resurrected unless they are dead first. So the self must die before the new life can begin.

To a dead person the coronavirus means absolutely nothing. The effect on the person is zero. And this reality is far deeper reaching. It changes everything about a person's life. They no longer live their lives, but Christ lives His life in them. Is Christ unsettled by the coronavirus? Totally not. Nothing surprises Jesus and nothing scares Him. Only when we die to ourselves can Christ's life be embodied and lived out in us.

3. *Taking up* the cross.

In Luke 9:23, Jesus does not hide the cost of discipleship. There is a personal cross each person must carry—it is not the cross of Jesus as it is often misquoted. To take up the cross is a conscious daily *choice* everyone has to make. The cross is not some physical, emotional, or mental torment one must live with—again, misinterpreted by some. It means to bear the shame, dishonor, criticism, suffering, and possible persecution on the Christian journey.

During this current strange situation, people will judge you and your church. Know that this is part of the package. If you take an objective Kingdom stance on the matter and refuse to be drawn in by all the media hype, they will criticize and ridicule you. You will pay the price. Your disciples will pay the price. But this is part of the norm, so expect it. Expect to be misunderstood especially by the world. They are in darkness and are even darkness. This is a way of life. It will happen again and again, not just with the coronavirus situation. Accept the cross. Take it daily and encourage those you lead to do the same.

4. A *daily* surrender.

In this same verse (Luke 9:23), Jesus reveals to us the key inside the key of discipleship. This *daily* aspect is the key to everything we do as disciples of Jesus. If something has been missed in discipleship, it is this key. Our supreme love for Jesus has to be a daily choice. Our surrender is to be daily. Our taking up the cross must be daily. Our following of Christ must be daily. Move from Sunday to daily. Make every day a Sunday, better yet, a Son-day!

It is tempting to move on to the next challenge Jesus brings, but we will not just yet. Let me emphasize what most believers know. As humans we operate best when we *habitually* do what we need to do. It takes about six weeks to develop a habit. We are to make the daily surrender a personal habit, then bring others to a place where they can do the same.

Jesus wants to be Emmanuel—God with us every day. Inasmuch as this is a challenge, it is also an invitation. He wants to provide for us daily, to live a life in the Spirit daily, to be in constant prayer and fellowship with Him. Once we can develop the habit of daily surrender, we create space in our most inner being for Christ to reign. We give up the steering wheel and we become the passenger of our body, mind, and will—our soul. Our ego is dead. We dealt with it first thing in the morning. We allow Christ to drive our life. We live life in the Spirit, filled by the Spirit, led by the Spirit, empowered by the Spirit, and anointed by the Spirit—just like Jesus lived His life. We become copies of Jesus! This is daily discipleship.

5.   A true *following* of Jesus.

My feeling is that many well-intended Christians are *fans* of Jesus. They associate with Christianity and even with Jesus quite well, but they don't want to truly identify with Him. They love His teachings, His blessings, and His provision. They even love the Sunday service and everything that comes with it. They are great supporters of Jesus. This is not what Jesus asks for. He is not looking for *fans*—He wants *followers*.

The invitation Jesus made was to follow Him in every true sense we can comprehend. He lived a life in full obedience to God, and so must we. He lived a life in the power of the Holy Spirit, and we are to do the same. We must walk as He walked, talk like He talked and do what He did. We are to copy, imitate, and replicate the Master in word and deed. We are to follow Him in serving others, washing their feet, praying for them, providing for them, healing them, restoring them and even dying for them, if need be.

There has to be proof we are followers of Jesus and there has to be fruit if we are led by the Lord's Spirit. I remember a story of a young man who received Christ in an outreach meeting while he was visiting a new town. Soon after praying, he chatted with the pastor who shared the gospel. He told the pastor that in his village there were no Christians and upon returning there he didn't know how he would live as a Christian. He wanted to know what to say, what to do, and how to live out his new identity. The pastor told him to return to his village and tell everyone he became a Christian. The people in his village would tell him how he ought to live. Humorous, but true.

The world already knows how a disciple of Jesus should live. The Christians are the ones who have yet to practise it daily, to shift from mere church-attending Christians to true followers of Jesus. This is what pure discipleship is all about.

6. A true *love for one another.*

There's no doubt that everything begins and ends with love when it comes to God, because that is His very nature. When we are born again, we are born from above and inherit His supernatural nature, which is characterized by real love.

No wonder one of the terms of being a disciple of Jesus is to love the brothers and sisters, as Jesus modeled it. He challenged us to love as a testimony of our true discipleship.

> *A new commandment I give to you, that you **love one another**: just as I have loved you, you also are to love one another. By this all people will know that you are my disciples, if you have love for one another* (John 13:34-35).

As disciples we are to obey our Master. When the Master commands, we execute. We do not discuss, negotiate, think about it, or look at options. We obey. We choose to love our brothers and sisters. This love is not based on their performance, their response, or their worth. Our ministry is unto Jesus. We love them because

He commanded us to do so. Train yourself not to negotiate loving them. Just do it.

When you do that, you are demonstrating that you are a disciple of Jesus. The world will notice. People will see and know that you are set apart, that you are of another world, that you have higher values, and that you belong to Jesus.

Many Christians want to testify to others about Jesus and they equip themselves with great teaching to do so. But how many of them have been obedient to this essential command of God to love one another? As Jesus loved us, we are to love one another, and then teach people to do the same. This is the basis of discipleship.

7. A genuine *forsaking* of everything.

If I haven't made you uncomfortable until now, this may just do it. Jesus did not hide the cost of following Him. Discipleship is costly.

> *In the same way, those of you who do not give up everything you have cannot be my disciples* (Luke 14:33 NIV).

A few months ago I went to Brisbane to visit one of our campus churches in Queensland to conduct a baptism. We chose a beautiful spot on the Gold Coast and lots of passersby had the chance to witness a beautiful expression of our Christian faith. A six-year-old girl approached me and asked me what it would cost to get baptized. She thought there was a price to pay to go in the water and get baptized. I didn't take her inquiry lightly. I told her it would cost her everything. She was puzzled to find it would cost that much. Of course I also explained in more depth to her understanding as well.

Unless we learn that following Jesus is an all-consuming matter where we give up everything, we can never truly follow Jesus. This is not a mistake in the Bible, nor is this an extreme demand.

Jesus is serious. We ought to be serious. He actually forbids us to store up treasure on earth (Matthew 6:19-20). Everything beyond our basic necessity must be invested into the Kingdom of God—be it missions, ministries, churches, schools, etc.

Why are we unsettled by the coronavirus? It is because it affects our earthly treasures. It exposes our resource management. Where have you been saving and storing your wealth? What about those you lead or minister to? What are they chasing every day? What do they spend their life and money on? Where are they placing their treasures? Is it bigger houses, newer cars, lavish holidays, extravagant dining out, fancy clothes, expensive shoes, or the latest digital electronics?

A disciple of Jesus acknowledges that everything comes from the Lord and is responsible for stewarding every dollar and every cent. The money comes from God, because our ability to earn it comes from Him. "...*What do you have that you did not receive? If then you received it, why do you boast as if you did not receive it?*" (1 Corinthians 4:7).

We've taught our people to tithe, and at best some do. Most don't. We haven't discipled them into stewarding it all for the Lord. We haven't taught them that in the New Covenant all belongs to God, not just 10 percent, and we are responsible for how we administer every cent.

When we have this perspective, it does not matter how much we have, it is how we manage what we have. And when challenges come, like the coronavirus, we are not affected because everything is God's, we are just managing His affairs on earth. Everything is Kingdom.

Jesus' Model of Discipleship Means *Maturity*

You can probably tell by now that this topic is very heavy on my heart. I have been encouraging and equipping the saints into discipleship as a central theme of my ministry. This has exposed me to various stages of maturity in discipleship. I didn't pay much attention to this aspect until someone asked me a critical question, "Natanael, when do you know you're a mature disciple of Jesus?"

The first temptation was to say, "When you are like Jesus!" But I immediately hesitated because almost everyone would tell me that no one is like Jesus. And if you did become like Jesus, what's next? You reached the peak of your being.

So I went into deep thinking here, acknowledging that our life is a journey of following the Lord—not a level we need to attain. But there had to be something that proves a vivid and tangible maturity level in disciples. The Spirit led me to Stephen, one of the disciples in the early church, as an example for spiritual maturity.

Let's pick up the story after his speech in Acts 7:55-60:

But he [Stephen], *full of the Holy Spirit, gazed into heaven and saw the glory of God, and Jesus standing at the right hand of God. And he said, "Behold, I see the heavens opened, and the Son of Man standing at the right hand of God." But they cried out with a loud voice and stopped their ears and rushed together at him. Then they cast him out of the city and stoned him. And the witnesses laid down their garments at the feet of a young man named Saul. And as they were stoning Stephen, he called out, "Lord Jesus, receive my spirit." And falling to his knees he cried out with a loud voice, "Lord, do not hold this sin against them." And when he had said this, he fell asleep.*

The following are examples of maturity in a disciple.

1. A mature disciple is full of the Holy Spirit (Acts 7:55). Not half measure, not occasionally, not just at church—fullness! This disciple is in the Spirit, feeds daily on the Word of God, and embodies the Godhead.

2. A mature disciple gazes into heaven (Acts 7:55). This disciple lives on earth but penetrates intently into the heavenly realms. Heaven is real and the mature disciple engages the divine dimension, focuses on heaven, and is unmoved by anything on earth. Nothing can take this person's eyes off Jesus.

3. A mature disciple sees the glory of God (Acts 7:55). This disciple has a deep awareness of God's glory, wants nothing else, is all consumed by bringing glory to God.

4. A mature disciple sees Jesus standing at the right hand of God (Acts 7:55). This disciple sees who Jesus is and how He ministers to us from heaven. This person's ministry is unto Jesus.

5. A mature disciple shares Jesus (Acts 7:56). This disciple shares the person of Jesus and the message of salvation, even to enemies.

6. A mature disciple lays his/her life down (Acts 7:59). This disciple holds nothing back and surrenders everything, even life itself.

7. A mature disciple forgives everyone (Acts 7:60). This disciple's love for people offers forgiveness even unto death.

This is what a maturing disciple does. The apostle Stephen's example seems extreme. It is. Jesus demands nothing less. Why? We are talking here of life and death, eternal life and eternal perishing. Losing one's life means gaining it.

This example reveals to us the secrets of a mature disciple. When the apostle Stephen penetrated into the heavens and saw the glory of God, he wanted nothing else. He reached the point of no return in his walk with the Lord. Mature disciples have reached the point of no return in their walk with God. It means that no matter what happens, they will never turn their back on Christ. They have become one with Christ, His bond slave. In life and in death they will not give in to sin or hatred. They spend time with and learn from the Master. They read and meditate on the Word, allowing this to become alive in them. They don't wait for Sunday spoon-feeding. They don't learn the gospel according to what they occasionally pick up along their Christian walk. They immerse themselves in the Word of God and need no external motivation in their Christian walk. They are self-governing, in effect, Christ-governing. They are already all sold out to Jesus. They have reached the point of no return—that is *mature discipleship.*

This is a litmus test for you first, then for those following or watching you. If you are to lead people through the coronavirus period, you need to reach this maturity and help them do the same. Bring yourself and others to this level of maturity and in the era ahead solidify this as the norm. Do not return to mere Christianity. Adopt mature discipleship as a way of life. This is the new normal Jesus brought two thousand years ago, and we are to embrace it.

Jesus Sends You to *Make Disciples*

Believers are familiar with the Great Commission as one of the most important commands of Jesus. It is, and we must rediscover it afresh:

> *And Jesus came and said to them, "All authority in heaven and on earth has been given to me. Go therefore and make disciples of all nations, baptizing them in the name of the Father and of the Son and of the Holy Spirit, teaching them to observe all that I have commanded you. And behold, I am with you always, to the end of the age"* (Matthew 28:18-20).

Discipleship was Jesus' method of spreading the gospel to the world. This method worked and is still working. Many believers are doing a great job at it and I commend you for obeying Jesus' command. But for many others, this is still work in progress.

Here's the Scripture passage breakdown.

1. Jesus in full authority is commanding us (Matthew 28:18). Jesus has received full authority in heaven and on earth and is *commanding* us with authority; but not only that, He is also passing this authority to us.

2. Make disciples (Matthew 28:19). The prerogative is to *make disciples.* The heart of the command is not to go, not to baptize or to teach—it is to make disciples. Make disciples by going, baptizing, and by teaching. The key of the command is to make disciples.

3. Make disciples of all nations (Matthew 28:20). To disciple a nation requires strategy and courage, unity, and purpose. *Every nation matters* in the eyes of God, every tribe and every group. Our cities are multiethnic. Start targeting these people groups to disciple them.

4. Teach them to obey everything (Matthew 28:20). Discipleship does not stop at baptism. It is a process that begins before salvation, carries through salvation, baptism, Holy Spirit filling, maturity, and then replication. New disciples need to be taught to observe and obey all that Jesus has commanded. This is where most of us fail. We teach to embrace, to accept, to even teach others—but first we must teach them to obey. We need to go the full cycle and then release them to do the same.

So why don't Christians make disciples?

1. Because they don't fully understand what discipleship is. Discipleship means following the Lord as a learner of Him, by doing life with Him and with others. When we disciple people, we must do life on life and to most people this is too intrusive. How can someone learn of us if we don't allow them into our lives? Jesus' model was a full immersion in His life.

2. Because they haven't been discipled themselves. This is the biggest *perceived* hurdle out there. Unfortunately this is a lame excuse used even by many leaders. It may be true that they haven't been discipled, but that is because they never seriously took on discipleship for themselves. Remember, we need to become disciples *of Jesus*, not of a leader. Having a leader is wonderful and needed, but we can be discipled by Jesus alone, too. It's time for us to be true disciples. It's time to lead ourselves well so we can lead others. We need to undergo the process first before we take others through it. You be the disciple you want others to be. And then become a disciple who disciples others.

3. Because they believe discipleship is for church leaders only. There's a myth that only church leaders can disciple others, so most people back off. Yet, Jesus says this is a command for everyone. This is not optional. Jesus commanded all of us to be disciples and make disciples.

The early church made disciples. Not merely saved Christians. I just did a count of the number of times the word "disciple" or its various forms appears in the book of Acts alone. I found it thirty-five times. Christian? In Acts 11:26 they are first called Christians. You would think that from this chapter onward Luke would refer to them as Christians. Not so. Twenty-one times after that, every time referenced those following Jesus and converting to Christianity, he used the term "disciple."

This is no mistake. The disciples of Jesus, later known as apostles, were not making converts. They were not making church members. They were not making saved people. They were making disciples, disciples of Jesus Christ. This is why the number of disciples multiplied so rapidly in the first century church. Everyone was making disciples.

Whether you are a church leader or leading your family, rediscover discipleship. The current situation with the coronavirus highlights the discipleship gap in our ministries. Believers should be people who stand strong during this test and every test the enemy throws at them. Discipleship means preparing them for life, a daily life with Christ and in Christ, a daily walk in the footsteps of the Master. Let's not return to church membership. Let's embrace discipleship!

ONE APPLICATION

1. What is the one application for your personal life when it comes to rediscovering discipleship?

2. What is the one application for your church that you can take on immediately?

CHAPTER 11

REFORM CHURCH GOVERNANCE

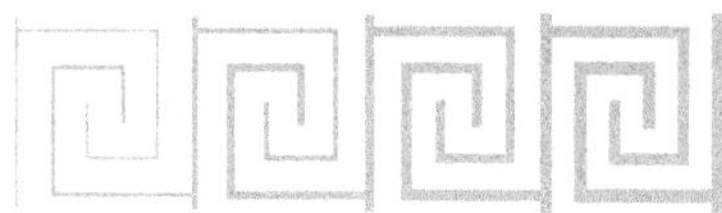

And he gave the apostles, the prophets, the evangelists, the shepherds and teachers, to equip the saints for the work of ministry, for building up the body of Christ.

—Ephesians 4:11-12

The Challenges

→ *Most church denominations have a nonbiblical, hierarchical governance structure.*

→ *The tendency for church leaders is to rule, not teach.*

→ *How can church leaders care for and lead people during the COVID-19 pandemic?*

→ *What is the reformation the church requires?*

I grew up in communist Romania in the 1970s and '80s and attended a traditional Pentecostal church in a small town of about 12,000 people. My father was an evangelist in our region and my grandfather was a Baptist church leader in his small village. Growing up with these mighty men of God gave me awareness and insights into what was going on in the church arena.

This period of history was marked by communism in the Eastern bloc of Europe. Communism is a political and economic doctrine, a high form of socialism that replaces private property with public ownership and state control. Dictatorship is the norm in a communist governance. Everything is top down, and everyone serves the leader of the government, the dictator. He is like a god of the nation and everyone almost bows to him. Everything is owned by the state and everyone works for state-run entities.

What was staggeringly interesting in this era in Romania is that the Protestant churches were given a democratic constitution and were deemed to be run as democratic entities. Even though they were highly controlled by the *securitatea* and the state, with spies in every church, they had to have democratic governance. The church members were voting on decisions and on the appointment of church leaders. The leaders were appointed by the congregation and vetted by the government. Most of them, unfortunately, became dictators themselves as this was the most common form of leadership they were accustomed to.

This means the church was the only democratic entity within the communist regime. Why did they want this? This was purposely allowed to create division and unrest in the church.

Most church arguments and unrests spring out of leadership elections and governance issues. This has happened throughout history and the communists knew this. So, they wanted to make sure the church would be unsettled from within. As such, they adopted the congregational democratic model for church governance in a communist nation. Bewildering.

What is even more astonishing is that thirty years after the communism curtain has fallen, and the church having the freedom to operate in any form of governance, it remains in the same model, with the same issues and facing the same challenges. It is a ruling model that does not work because it's not biblical.

Why am I telling you this story? I am telling you because we don't seem to learn from history.

The coronavirus pandemic has caught the church worldwide by surprise and revealed some of the underlying issues that have either been ignored or not revisited for a long time. The church was not ready for it. Church leaders were nowhere near prepared for a shake such as this. And questions need to be asked all the way to the top, in fact, from the top down.

The show could not go on. Church buildings were locked for at least two months; and because the church was dependent on its political structure and it could no longer operate that way, many people felt abandoned.

Most churches hadn't done a self-check on how they were structured, so they focused quickly to move to an online show hoping the flock would be catered for in this virtual way. This worked to some extent; but in reality, down deep, there's evidence of underlying issues.

The pandemic unsettled people everywhere and Christians were not spared. Most Christians are church-dependent, spoon-fed on Sunday, and ill-equipped to sustain their Christian walk without the church meeting. Is there something wrong with how church governance is undertaken? Are we to return to the way things were—or should we take this opportunity to revisit how the church is governed.

Where Did the Church Go Wrong?

When it comes to church governance there are three main models that have been traditionally accepted in churches. One: There's the Episcopal model with presiding bishop/archbishop councils. Two: There is the Presbyterian model with oversight and authority in the hands of the elders. Three: And in the last century, there's the

Congregational model with the leadership in the democratic voting hands of the church members.

The Congregational model is probably the widest model used in the modern church, and it is similar to how secular corporate companies are run. The hierarchy contains the board or the council, then the senior pastor or chief executive officer (CEO), followed by ministry leaders and staff. The power and the risk belong to the people in the congregation, and the leadership is accountable to the congregation.

Other models are emerging more and more as some churches explore the early church's simple governance model.

Why is there such diversity in church government, especially in the modern church? It is because the Bible does not offer a definitive structure model, but it does reveal how governance *should* work out. It covers areas such as the offices of apostles, prophets, evangelists, pastors, and teachers; the role of bishops and deacons; and the role of elders. More so, it gives a set of criteria by which leaders' character and qualifications are to be measured. For our discussion here, however, the focus is on governance, not on the selection criteria.

The church should be an organic entity, as it was from the beginning. It has subsequently been organized and institutionalized into something that does not resemble its beginnings at all. The church has created for itself institutions, denominations, and structures that are not biblically found, and most church leaders are not even aware of why they are in those structures and what they mean.

And in the midst of all this, we are hit by a pandemic that shakes all structures, leaving us with more questions than answers:

- What will happen to our church members?
- How will they be cared for?
- Who will teach them?
- Who will pastor them?

- Will they participate in the digital platforms?
- Can our current leadership structure reach out to them?
- Can we handle church this way?
- How long can we maintain this?
- Are there better ways?
- What does history teach us?
- What does the Bible teach us?
- How was the first century church operating and expanding without buildings?
- Was their success based on strategy or governance or both?
- If governance, what was their governance like?
- Is this something we should revisit?
- Do we need to reform our church governance?
- Do we have the courage to ask these big questions?
- Do we have the courage to engage in a reformation?

The current crisis should take us back to the early church to see what blueprint they were using that allowed them to thrive during all the persecution and challenges they faced in the first centuries.

The Silent Reformation

There is a silent reformation happening in the church today. In this reformation the return is not to the pre-COVID-19 norm but to even older norms.

Believers are seeking God, more of God! They are looking for something genuine, for a relationship that is real. People are tired of the usual, the predictable, and the busy programs we persuade them week in week out to attend. More so, they are done with institutions and denominations. They want the real deal.

Most of our churches rely on business-type governance, management, and marketing to run. We have created sensitive, client-seeker churches. They are consumer oriented. The focus is on how we *do* church rather than how we *are* the church.

Crisis gives us an opportunity to revisit and reflect on everything. And we can start at the top. We can also go back to the very beginning of church history to learn again what we have lost along the way.

How simple was church governance in the first century church! An apostle would go into a city and begin a house church. The church was known as a city church that began to meet in many houses. The apostle would raise up elders and shepherds who would look after the flock (Acts 14:22-23). He would then leave them to carry on the ministry in their city and he would go to another city to do the same work over again. He would visit them occasionally or write to them to ensure they remained true to the faith and offered apostolic cover for them.

Some churches had apostles—Jerusalem, Judea, Caesarea—and others had visiting apostles or founding apostles. Their leadership was simple. The elders were part of a plurality leadership, of equal collaboration and understanding.

There was an *order* but not a *hierarchy* in the early church. The order began with apostles, then prophets, then teachers, and then the other functions and giftings (1 Corinthians 12:28).

Most churches today operate on pastor and teacher leadership. Out of the five functions Jesus gave the church—apostles, prophets, evangelists, pastors and teachers—churches today operate on only two. It's like running on two cylinders when you have five. At best, even if there is a fivefold ministry governance, it is usually seen through pastoral lenses. This means churches have teaching pastors, shepherding pastors, evangelistic pastors, prophetic pastors, and apostolic pastors. What is wrong with this? Well, all is seen through pastoral lenses, and as such it all is *shepherding leadership* and not *strategic leadership.* It means that most of the leadership is focusing on *caring* and *teaching* the flock rather than *equipping* it strategically for ministry.

The apostle Paul explained the purpose for the fivefold ministry: *"And he* [Jesus] *gave the apostles, the prophets, the evangelists, the shepherds and teachers, to **equip the saints** for the work of ministry, **for building up the body of Christ"** (Ephesians 4:11-12).

The purpose of the five functions was to *equip the saints* for the work of ministry, to build up the body of Christ. What were the five-fold to do? Equip. Prepare. Train. Perfect. Who was to do the work of ministry, the work of service, the work of serving or the work of ministration? The saints—every member of the church. Do we truly believe in the priesthood of all believers? Do we embrace it as a prac-tice of the church today? Do we equip every man and every woman in their priestly calling? If so, our churches would be different. The result of our equipping would ripple through. And, as promised, the body of Christ would be built up!

If the body of Christ is not being built up during this crisis period, it is because we haven't practiced these simple verses of instruction from Jesus. Any other structure of leadership cannot build up the body. This formula will work for any given situation, in any time of history. It is *Christ given.*

Jesus gave the fivefold ministry for church *leadership* and for church *maturity.* The fivefold is an equipping ministry. Most people in church today believe it is the pastors' job to do the work of min-istry. Not so. It is their role to equip the members, who should be disciples as such, to do the ministry. That is why we need a reforma-tion! And silently, praise God, this is happening in many churches.

How is it happening? Leaders are realizing that if the Lord gave apostles first, this function must be *coming back* into the church today. It is a function needing restoration. A large number of churches believe the role of the apostle, and in some cases of the prophet, ceased with the death of the twelve apostles. And they have lost this primary and essential function from leadership.

In the same way, most churches do not have the prophet function in their leadership. They may even accept prophecies but have not restored this function in their church. Some ignore it totally believing both the prophetic function and prophecies ceased long ago. What self-robbing and church-robbing thinking!

If we are to embrace the biblical model of the fivefold, we would look at it through the apostolic order of 1 Corinthians 12:28. We would then have apostolic apostles, apostolic prophets, apostolic evangelists, apostolic pastors (or shepherds), and apostolic teachers. The lenses would be apostolic for every function rather than pastoral as it is in most modern churches today.

Imagine if churches were *reformed* to this early church governance! Imagine apostles equipping people in the apostolic ministry. Imagine prophets training the body in prophetic ministry. Imagine evangelists preparing people for evangelism. Imagine pastors equipping the flock in pastoring one another. Imagine teachers equipping others to teach.

If we simply did all this, our churches would be alive and well through any crisis—and ready to stand and minister in any situation. The COVID-19 pandemic caught the church unprepared, but it is teaching us a lesson. It is bringing us back to the original blueprint to *reassess* and *reform*.

When all fivefold ministries equip, we have a body who ministers, who builds itself up, who grows, who matures, and who births. We have a church that withstands anything. We have an army of believers who can not only walk the Christian walk but can also serve in their community throughout all the challenges their community faces. We have mature disciples who disciple others. The whole church fabric is healthy because there are healthy threads throughout.

Why isn't this governance model embraced? It is not embraced because it is not attractive to most leaders today. Worldly structures are top down. Church structures are top down. To flatten the leadership is to unsettle the senior pastor, and most senior leaders are not prepared to accept this. It is uncomfortable to share leadership. It may be accepted as a teaching and as a principle, but not attractive to be implemented. It is challenging to adopt a renewed mindset toward this change. Top leaders have to accept it first, then the ripple effect will be revolutionary.

Leaders, it starts with us! Let's not just nod our heads in approval. Let's not just teach it, as I know many of us have done. Let's put it into practice. You and I begin this. It starts with me and it starts with you.

The Simplicity of Biblical Governance

Biblical governance is simple. It has been made complex but it shouldn't be. What we simply need is to go back to the original. We need to go back to Jesus, to the leadership He gave to His church. We need a restoration of the fivefold. We need to appoint Christ as the Senior Leader of our church—not just say it. We need a restoration of apostles and prophets. We need a church governance reformation.

The following is biblical church governance in its most simplistic form:

1. *Christ is the Head of the church (Ephesians 5:23).* Not the bishop, not the senior pastor, not the pope, nor the local pastor. It is Christ. Alone. Until He becomes the senior figure in your church, you will limit what your church can become.

2. *Holy Spirit is the Guide of the church, both universal and individual (John 16:7-14).* He comforts, helps, guides, convicts, teaches and declares. Until your church is led by the Holy Spirit, you will be relying on manmade strategies that produce dead works.

3. Elders are the leaders for each individual church (Acts 14:23). They operate in the fivefold functions of apostles, prophets, evangelists, teachers, and pastors to equip the saints to do the work of ministry (Ephesians 4:11-12). Until your church reforms its governance to the biblical model, there will be a divisive power struggle and the body will never become mature in serving. Elders mature the saints into ministry. They are the equippers of the saints to do the work. They are the overseers. They are the disciple makers and teach those to make disciples themselves. There is no hierarchy. It's flat. There is order but not hierarchy.

An Opportunity to Reform

You are invited, as terrifying as this may seem, to be a revolutionary and a reformist. Ask yourself and your leadership the tough questions. You will be faced with some disruptive answers. You will be led to some of the greatest truths a Christian leader can discover. And you can lead in a revolutionary way through any confronting challenges and through any unsettling period of history. You will mature the bride for her King.

ONE APPLICATION

1. What is the one shift you will personally make today that changes everything?

2. What is the one shift you will apply in your church that will revolutionize everything?

REINVENT IN THE DIGITAL ERA

To the weak I became weak, that I might win the weak.
I have become all things to all people,
that by all means I might save some.

—1 Corinthians 9:22

The Challenges

→ *The church is forced to find nonphysical ways to connect with its people.*

→ *The digital world is waiting for the church to embrace it.*

→ *The church needs to reinvent itself in the digital space.*

→ *The church of the future will have a strong digital presence.*

As soon as the COVID-19 hit to the degree of the whole world being kept in isolation, I began praying about our people, and also the church at large, to become aware of the opportunity to have a prayer closet (Matthew 6:6), an inner room or a war room in each home.

I then created a group on Facebook called "in the closet," and within a few days it grew to 500 members, and in less than three weeks to over 1,000 members. Every day I place a short post to encourage the group members and I also invite filtered contribution.

If I had attempted to create a group like this a few months before the lockdown, I would have struggled to populate it. But now, the world has rapidly changed including the Christian world.

The restrictions placed on the church to close their buildings and cease assemblies has brought about one of the most amazing openings to the digital world. Both church organizations and groups and individuals have made use of the digital world to broadcast services, teachings, worship songs, and testimonies.

Opportunities for Churches to Embrace Digital Communication

Crises shift us. They disrupt us. They prompt us. They accelerate us. They make us do things we previously thought about doing but were delayed or put off. The coronavirus forced us into some church of the future that is rapidly shaping up, almost overnight. The apostle Paul understood the importance of adjusting and adapting quickly. He became all things to all people so he could "save some" (1 Corinthians 9:22). We need to use all available means to connect with as many people as possible—to save them and to serve them. And we need to get going in this digital space quickly. The following are some major lessons we need to quickly learn.

1. The Internet is a front door, not a back door. When we launched the Australian School of Ministry as an online school in 2015, we were told that it would not work. People were telling us that ministries, mainly churches, that had services online were losing people through the back door. Their argument was that people don't have the discipline to be committed and engaged in online churches. They were wrong. Our students were thriving and they still are.

We embraced technology when we began planting churches, too. From day one when we opened every Menora Church, we were broadcasting live. We had hundreds of views on a regular basis, even though only 25-35 people were physically present in the church building.

The world is online and it lives online. Our purpose is to win the world back to Christ. If we're not engaging online, we are missing the very people we are trying to reach. It is so much easier for someone to check out a church online than physically come through the door on Sunday.

In Australia, fewer and fewer church buildings are approved in residential suburbs, and there is a planning shift toward commercial areas. The crossroads corner sites that were the norm sites for church buildings in the last few centuries have become extremely expensive. The church does not have the physical real estate presence in the community it once enjoyed. Internet space has created an even playing field. There are opportunities to become much more visible to your community online than you would ever be with a physical building presence.

The rapid shut down of the church buildings through the coronavirus pandemic forced the church in an accelerated move toward online.

In a period of history when most people measure the success of a church by the number of bums on seats, what would it take for us to value those who join us digitally? Maybe it's time to renew our thinking and include those who join us on the Internet and engage with them, also. I believe they are waiting for an invitation to be involved, to contribute and to be part of the extended church family. Yes, there will be some who only consume and casually drop in on your interface. But many will be ready to jump onboard to fellowship and be equipped. And remember that you can now do this daily, not just on Sundays.

2. Church can be done every day, not only on Sunday. We've never had so many digital meetings during the week as we do now. We used to pack most things into the Sunday. We now have Monday prayer, Tuesday leadership development, Wednesday Bible study, Friday youth chat, and on Sunday a few live broadcasted services. The connection with the church is now a daily encounter. We have several groups on various platforms and there is so much daily interaction both between leaders and the church, and between the church members.

We have also encouraged families in our church to come together on a daily basis for a moment of prayer, worship, and Word reflection. This family devotion is now becoming more and more a real way of doing church outside church, on a daily basis. This should not be a new thing, but for many people it is. The current situation triggered this spiritual desire, and it is wonderful to know they're engaging in it.

Will Sunday still have a role in the season ahead? Absolutely. I miss our Sunday celebration. I miss public gatherings, and I do believe in them. The current reality, though, tells us that people will not just want to return to the Sunday expression. They have tasted more, and Sunday may no longer be the *main* thing everyone does anymore.

It has been a Christian cliché to say that our ministry should be outside the walls of the church; but the reality is or at least was, that our behavior demonstrated otherwise. We embraced the Monday to Friday ministry at the mind level, but did not allow it to sink into our hearts. We thought it was a great idea, but we hardly ever engaged in it.

Now the church has to realize that people need hope, encouragement, and teachings every day. Our people need the church to come alongside them every day. They need to be uplifted and propelled to live out their faith every day. And in recent weeks, we were forced to do that in an unprecedented way.

As a leader, I am already thinking about the season ahead. And I am asking myself some meaningful questions: Am I committed to carry on the new daily digital connection with the church after the lockdown, or will I revert to our old ways? Will I be too tired to keep it going on daily basis as I do now? Will our people's interest wane or will they have the expectation that this is the new norm? Can we improve our online presence? Can we become more visible to the world out there through digital platforms? Can we take the church to an everyday engagement, not just a weekend celebration?

3. Churches can run better on less resources. I may not make too many friends here, especially church leaders. Most of the church budget goes on buildings and personnel. It is time to see how the digital platforms can assist us in optimizing church expenses, especially our staffing.

The current lockdown has brought us back into the homes and most of our work is now done online. Most church offices are now empty and the church is surviving, even thriving. This tells us that our office buildings (or offices in the buildings), are not as vital as we thought. Even before the coronavirus, 80-90 percent of our church's real estate was not used throughout the week.

Our staff can work from home. They can engage remotely. We can have meetings online. We can be more productive on less resources.

This is also a good time to look at the way we prioritize technology, both in our running of the church (admin) and our interaction with the church members. There is a large palette of apps ready to make our world so much simpler. We can automate most of our tasks. We can simplify and optimize most of our admin and communication tasks. We can even have our own church app through a simple, affordable monthly subscription.

Our online presence also needs a conscious review. We must accept that the online church is just as real as is everything else we daily engage in online, like shopping online. We may have resisted this for a while, but today's reality brought this message home very quickly.

Churches spend the most money for in-person experiences, allocating very little for our online expression. The set up and running of our online platforms is generally passed on to some teenage volunteers who squeeze it in between their weekly studies and part-time jobs. The church of the future that has just become the church of today, needs to reevaluate the importance of their online presence, and do it quickly.

Our budget allocation needs to focus on our online presence. We need to look for qualified staff to take on this new role and to do it exceedingly well. We need to invest in technology to produce high quality content and have it uploaded and distributed in a real time way. It may be that a high proportion of our budget (in some cases up to 50 percent) will go toward our online church.

Everyone we want to reach and influence is already *waiting for us online.* If you look at the way you do life now, you'll see that the first place you go to inquire about anything, is online. Before you choose your holiday destination, you look online. Before you make purchases, you look online. Before you hire someone, you look at their digital footprint on social media. Even dating begins online for many people.

When reaching out to people about our church, what do we do? We send them a link to our website or to our church's service on a video platform or to some blog or podcast from our online platform. It's the way we introduce the church family to them. It's the way we take the conversation further with simple discipleship tools (teachings, videos, courses, regular meetings, etc.). It is the way we connect with people and stay connected. It is the way we plug them into the online community and gradually into our home groups and our Sunday celebration. And all this starts and continues online.

As you are reading this, and if you are a church leader, you may be somewhat concerned about *giving*. The church has taught its people to come prepared on Sundays with their tithes and offerings and to gracefully place their gifts in the collection bag, plate, bucket, whatever. Our culture has changed and our cash behavior has changed. People carry less and less cash and some do not carry cash or even a checkbook at all anymore. Even if the people attending church want to be generous, unless we have a digital payment portal, they cannot give.

The church has to adapt quickly to the electronic way of giving and create simpler and faster ways for people to engage in giving. We strongly encourage our church family to make recurring weekly or monthly payments of their tithes in the church account. This alleviates pressure or worry if or when they have given, and it helps the church with budgeting.

4. Churches can have more impact, faster. It's time to come to grips with the simple fact that the digital world can take us to the world out there much faster and with far greater impact.

The churches that didn't understand this until now, and only in this crisis were forced to adopt digital technology, will discover the scale of their impact. Initially they might have thought about embracing online presence only until the church goes back to "normal," but soon realized an online presence has opened new opportunities and new ways to impact the world.

It is far easier to reach people through the Internet than it is in real life. And this is an accepted way of introduction that leads to real-life connections.

Let's look at the YouVersion app's story. It's a Bible app launched in 2017, and at the time this book is being written, the app had been downloaded and installed more than 400 million times! It was started by a local church and is still being run by a small team at a local church.

Just the other day I filmed a short three minute live update on our soft return to normal here in Australia, and within a day it had been viewed over 2,000 times. And it was simply done with my phone.

5. *Church can be more creative online.* The first tendency when the church was forced to run online services, was to recreate the Sunday experience for its people.

The filming was done in church and the motions were exactly as the church used to do it when people were there. The welcome was almost the same, the four worship songs the same, the announcements, and then the pulpit preaching with some prayer at the end—all the same. The team dressed up and performed as they would with a crowd in front of them, and so did the pastor. We haven't transformed ourselves much. We haven't really come closer to our audience. We kept it predictable with not much engaging. We hadn't explored the creativity for doing things a bit differently.

But now we can be more intimate. Pastors can sit when they share. We can have a different way of worshipping. We don't need a full band. We can worship from our homes. We can preach from our study or outside on the front porch. We can have discussions. We can have forums. We can be so much more creative!

Many churches who broadcast services online now have an interactive side-bar box where viewers can post comments in real time—engaging and encouraging each other while listening to the message by the senior pastor. Sometimes urgent prayer requests are also posted. Leadership and other ministry pastors monitor the comments and respond to the prayer requests, and also provide lively and friendly interaction with viewers.

Open up to the possibilities! Let creativity flow. This is an amazing opportunity to think outside the building, outside the program, outside the service, and outside the norm. Be the church everywhere and show it. Use your phone camera and film it. Be real. Be intimate. Be insightful. And, please be short. The attention span online is lower, so keep things short and sweet, dynamically engaging and thought provoking.

Opportunities for Families and Individuals to Connect and Interact Online

Because of current digital technology, the world is more connected now than in any other time in history. Through our smart phones we can be connected to everyone we know and can not only talk to them but also see them in real time. Video chats are the norm and creating photo collages and edited videos are at the fingertip of every person.

What I love about this period is how some families have embraced the digital tools and have become very creative in engaging with other family members, friends, and the wider circles. Not only that, they have begun engaging with the wider viewers in sharing their faith. Many believers post images and videos of daily devotionals, family worship, creative singing, Bible reflections, and Christ-filled life moments. Never before in history have I seen so many Christians posting wonderful testimonial content on social media. Christians seem to be awakened to a new world. It's fascinating to see.

I love how individuals and families have risen to the occasion. I love how quickly they adjusted and have allowed their Spirit-filled creativity to shine. I love the boldness they display in sharing their faith in simplicity and authenticity. I enjoy watching them having the freedom to portray the Kingdom of God in various artistic expressions.

Many are taking the opportunity to interact with others anywhere in the world. They call family members for video chats and interact on a deeper level with friends and acquaintances.

They share their joy, laughter, and tears. They produce wonderful content that blesses so many people.

The audience reached through the social media and other digital channels is staggering. Every believer can become influential very quickly. We can touch so many lives in the virtual space like never before.

Our engagement is needed "out there," and I pray that we don't stop what we have begun. It may be tempting to think there are too many people posting, or to measure everything by the number of views or the ratings received. Please know this—nothing returns void in the Kingdom economics. Every seed you plant has the potential to bear fruit. So, plant on every field, every page, every channel, just keep sowing. There will be harvest, there will be a reaping.

God said through Isaiah: *"So shall My word be that goes forth from My mouth; it shall not return to Me void, but it shall accomplish what I please, and it shall prosper in the thing for which I sent it"* (Isaiah 55:11 New King James Version). Believe it.

Opportunities for the Season Ahead

When this is over, there will be many churches attempting to return to the way things were before. The temptation will be there for the predictable and the comfortable, ignoring the digital connection. My prayer is that yours will not be one of those churches!

Please understand me. I am not advocating to move to an online church and discard or minimize the physical gatherings. Far from it. What we are realizing in this season is that we have to do both. We have to be the church in our village, town, and city—and also in the world. We have to have a local physical presence and a worldwide online presence. We are to utilize every means to share the gospel and to be on every platform where we can engage with people.

Why is this? It is because this period of isolation has highlighted to us the possibilities the digital world offers. We are no longer limited by anything except the limits we place on ourselves. We can seamlessly reach local believers, and we can just as easily reach the wider community.

Because we are to be the salt of the earth (Matthew 5:13), we are to give taste to the world by every means possible. The church is often hurt by the immorality the media bombards us with. We have a responsibility to bring a divine moral Christian view into that sphere. We must have an impact in every space, including the virtual.

The years ahead will be years of advancement in technology. The church of the future will be a church with many open and interactive portals. Every industry will be pushing for new technology, and our digital world is constantly and rapidly emerging. The Spirit wants to lead us in this space to be at the tip of the arrow, to make use of every new technology to reach the world. If you have reinvented yourself, your church, and your ministry in the digital space, great. But realize that you need to keep reinventing. Embrace the digital era and the exciting period ahead.

ONE APPLICATION

1. What is the one reinvention you will personally make in the digital segment?

2. What reinvention will you take on for your church in the digital space?

CHAPTER 13

RELEASE THE POWER OF TOUCH

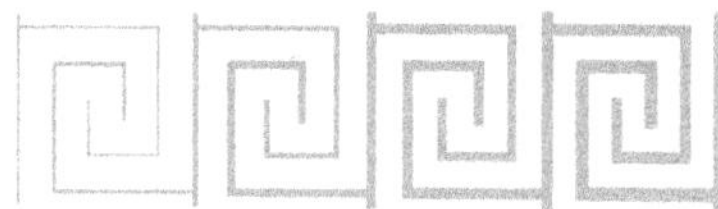

*Moved with pity, he [Jesus] stretched out his hand
and touched him and said to him, "I will; be clean."*

—Mark 1:41

The Challenges

→ *The pandemic is starving humanity of one its most elementary sensory need, the need for touch.*

→ *The human touch is our instinctive language that solidifies communication.*

→ *Christianity is a touch-based relationship and is now withheld from practicing it.*

→ *Post pandemic, the church will play a vital role in reestablishing the touch connection.*

A few years ago I visited a friend who was wheelchair bound due to multiple sclerosis and whose elderly mother was caring for him. She was in her early nineties; and because hardly anyone visited them in their small unit, she wouldn't always dress up or do her hair. We had a long chat about her life and the challenges she went through when she first migrated to Australia from Croatia in the 1950s.

Before I left, I leaned down toward my friend's mother who was sitting in an armchair, gave her a gentle kiss on her forehead, as my dad taught me, and a meaningful, unrushed hug. As I stood up, tears began to flow from her eyes. She said, "Natanael, it's been over ten years since someone kissed me."

I will never forget her. It was one of those moments that took my breath away and for a few seconds time just stopped. We call it a *kairos* moment. It messed me up for good. I never understood the power of a touch until them. What a simple kiss on a forehead can do! What a ten second purposeful hug can do!

The coronavirus pandemic has taken away from us one of the most essential of human needs, the need to touch and be touched. *Social distancing* means no handshakes, no hugs, and no cheek kisses. It is anything *but* social. A better term would be physical distancing. Now, more than ever, the human touch is what we crave. Two of Abraham Maslow's hierarchy of basic needs have to do with the human touch—safety and belonging.

The Immeasurable Power of Touch

When a baby is born, the child is placed immediately on the mother's breast and skin for bonding. The connection in those first seconds and minutes of life is life transforming for both the mother and the baby. Touch is the first sense developed as humans. The baby's first language after birth is touch, and they respond instantly to skin-to-skin contact. It is the secret weapon for a lifetime of successful relationships. Bonding gives babies security, trust, love, and care. No wonder why the first hour after birth is called the "golden hour." It also promotes the development of connections between brain cells that are critical for learning.

Mothers experience changes in their brain chemistry as they give birth characterized by an increase desire to nurture. As the baby begins to breastfeed, hormones that cause the uterus to contract and stop bleeding are instantly released. The uninterrupted deep connection with their baby in the first hour is critical for the child's development and for the mother's recovery.

The mother-baby connection is so strong that most babies don't even realize they are a separate human being until they begin to walk. They don't have a self-existential awareness. They are so close to the mother, especially if they are breastfed, that they believe they are still one body with her.

As children grow, skin-to-skin contact promotes cognitive benefits and trust for human relationships. The human connection is a touch connection. We feel more connected when we touch. Touch solidifies lasting impact and well-being in us. Without touch people are lonely, and loneliness leads to illness and inevitably to early death. Medical studies have proven that physical touch boosts our immune system, improves our psychological state, and can literally save lives. The human touch is powerful, essential, and everyone longs for it.

There is a beautiful story in the Bible of a woman who captured the amazing healing power released by Jesus through touching:

And behold, a woman who had suffered from a discharge of blood for twelve years came up behind him and touched the fringe of his garment, for she said to herself, "If I only touch his garment, I will be made well." Jesus turned, and seeing her he said, "Take heart, daughter; your faith has made you well." And instantly the woman was made well (Matthew 9:20-22).

This lady had an amazing faith in Jesus, that His touch would bring healing. She reasoned in her mind that if she could only touch Him, she would be healed. And instantly she was healed.

Jesus knew her situation and her desperation. Under Jewish law she was untouchable, not for a few days or a week, but for twelve years. She was deprived of human touch for twelve years! More so, her touching a Rabbi would make Him ceremoniously unclean. Everything she touched became unclean. It was almost like having COVID-19. She had a responsibility not to contaminate others.

Yet she had the faith and the courage to step out on a limb and touch Jesus! She was hoping no one would see her, that is why she sneaked behind Him. The risk was massive because everyone knew her situation. Her whole life was at stake. She was desperate for the healing that would not only heal her but also restore her as a dignified woman in society, and most likely as a wife and mother.

How powerful was this touch for her! And it wasn't even Jesus touching her, it was her touching Jesus' garment. But that touch of Jesus' cloth restored her to the human touch she was starved of for twelve long and emotionally painful years. In Luke's record of the event Jesus asks about who touched Him in such a way that *power* came out of Him (Luke 8:46). Her touch-power called upon Jesus' touch-power. Do you see the touch connection? Do you see the power released through the connection?

That touch made her well, it didn't just heal her. All three Gospel accounts say that she was made well, not merely healed. That very touch transformed her whole being. It was a holistic wellness. That touch totally cleansed her. That touch fully restored her in society. That touch utterly dignified her. That touch was the most powerful touch she ever experienced.

Skin Hunger Is Real

Mother Teresa told us that there is more hunger for love and appreciation in this world than for bread. Lack of affection can have negative effects on humans just like lack of food or water.

It is called *skin hunger*. People deprived of human touch are less happy, more lonely, are more likely to experience stress and depression, and have worse health in general. This is another need we need to be aware of.

Our skin is the largest organ in our body. The sense of touch develops in the womb before any other senses, and it never turns off. This touch sense exists long after our other senses have failed in old age. We enjoy the human touch, yet most likely, we never think of it until it is taken away.

The church has to realize what we're experiencing right now is a shift away from each other, and thus from the human touch. Social distancing is now en-masse. It is not just if people are feeling sick. It is 1.5 meters worldwide, no matter what! Never in history has humanity been asked to segregate this way on this scale. This has a massive impact on all of us; and we, as a church need to be consciously aware of this change in basic behavior.

The world is different. Most buildings you enter from now on will welcome you with sanitizer or disinfectant stands. Churches will have them, too. Handshakes may take a long time to return and hugs could be hard to get. Human behavior is different. It's a reality that cannot be ignored.

This is also an amazing opportunity for the church to shine. We are an embracing mob who sees beyond the pandemic and into the depth of our essential needs. We have an assignment ahead to reestablish the human touch as a nonthreatening expression of human connection.

Christianity Is Touchy

Christianity is family. When we become followers of Christ we enter His family and God is our Father. As family members, we have a sense of closeness, and touch is an important component of family life.

Handshakes, hugs, arms over the shoulder, pats on the back, high-fives, and helping hands are all part of our family life. We also have touch ministries in the church family. We lay hands on the sick and on people we minister to.

Christianity is a love relationship, a love of God and a love of others. Everyone knows that the church is a place where love is manifested and those who come to church have an expectation to be loved and cared for. Now this is not always real in many churches, but it should be.

Reclaim this ministry in your church as soon as the restrictions are lifted. Restore this as soon as you can. Start with your family and with your church family. Encourage everyone to reignite the touch connection. Everyone needs this. This is what Christianity is about. This is how Jesus taught us.

Jesus, a Physically Affectionate Liberator

Jesus intentionally used tactile methods in His ministry. The Gospels describe Him as a toucher. There are multiple cases in which our Savior reached out and embraced people when He could have just simply nodded, or just uttered some words. Let's look at a few instances.

1. Healing the leper.

In Jesus' days, leprosy was common and those infected had to be isolated from their community. If a leper was in close proximity to healthy people, he had to call out, "Unclean!" so others could avoid him (Leviticus 13:45-46). Oftentimes infected people could be without human touch for months or years. Jesus comes on the scene and is moved with compassion.

> *And a leper came to him* [Jesus], *imploring him, and kneeling said to him, "If you will, you can make me clean."*

Moved with pity, he stretched out his hand and touched him and said to him, "I will; be clean." And immediately the leprosy left him, and he was made clean (Mark 1:40-42).

Jesus could have healed the man in many ways, but He chose to heal him by touching him. Jesus wasn't just dealing with his illness, He was dealing with the man's isolation and rejection too. Jesus' touch assured both physical healing and social acceptance.

Our lesson is that we have the Christ-given ability to extend God's love, His grace, and His compassion through a gentle touch that conveys care, love, dignity, and value. The human touch can show people our care and concern, and provides a way to minister to them.

2. Laying hands on children.

Jesus' ministry on earth was jam-packed with teachings, healings, and miracles; and toward the end of His ministry, He gives us another deep insight into how important it is to bless our children. This did not seem of importance to His disciples and they even scolded people for bringing their children to Jesus. But Jesus was doing something significant here. He invited the little ones to come into His arms to be blessed by the laying on of His hands.

And they were bringing children to him [Jesus] that he might touch them, and the disciples rebuked them. But when Jesus saw it, he was indignant and said to them, "Let the children come to me; do not hinder them, for to such belongs the kingdom of God. Truly, I say to you, whoever does not receive the kingdom of God like a child shall not enter it." **And he took them in his arms and blessed them, laying his hands on them** *(Mark 10:13-16).*

Why is this story so significant? It is full of significance because what Jesus communicated through blessing and laying His hands on them was that the children belong to the Kingdom of God. He communicated their identity.

Throughout the Old Testament fathers blessed their children by laying hands on them. This tradition was vital to a child's identity. The father's blessing through touch was foundational to the child's development.

Our lesson as Christians is to teach people, especially fathers, to release God's blessing over their children by laying hands on them and pronouncing life-giving words. This needs to be an ongoing practice in our homes, highlighted more so now during this coronavirus segregation.

As spiritual fathers and mothers, we are to do the same for our spiritual sons and daughters. The son and daughter blessing solidifies over and over again their identity, which is what their lives are built upon.

3. Allowing John a resting place.

For the apostle John, the defining moment of his life was when Jesus allowed him to lean back against His chest during the last supper. That body-to-body touch speaks of how close Jesus allowed His disciples to come to Him.

> *One of the disciples, the one Jesus loved dearly, was reclining against him, his head on his shoulder* (John 13:23 The Message Bible).

Jesus allowed John to come and rest on Him at the table. Remember, Jesus first called them disciples, then friends, and then sons. Sons and daughters have a right at the father's chest, for assurance, affirmation, and comfort.

John embraced his identity in Christ and even called himself the disciple "whom Jesus loved." Did Jesus love him more than others?

No, but because John's love for Jesus was so great, he always drew near to Him and became His armor-bearer.

This touchy closeness made John the only disciple present at Jesus' crucifixion and also the first disciple to recognize the resurrected Jesus. John's gospel and letter writings are immersed in love because he allowed himself to be loved by Jesus and to love Him back.

As a man and a pastor, I have had the opening to minister to men in various circles, to bless them, to pray over them, to hug them, and even to let them cry on my shoulder or at my chest. This is godly interaction and we need to become comfortable to minister this way.

4. Presenting God as a loving Father who hugs and kisses.

When Jesus told His disciples the prodigal son story, He was giving them a glimpse of what the heavenly Father is like.

The younger son in the story wants to take his inheritance and leave his father to go to a faraway country and live on his own terms. Heartbroken, the father lets him go and the young man destroys his inheritance in reckless living. He ends up in desperate need and the best work he could get was caring for pigs. He realizes his mistake, repents, and wants to return home. He knows that being with his father, even as a servant, is better than being away. As such, the young son returns home:

> *And he arose and came to his father. But while he was still a long way off, his father saw him and felt compassion, and ran and embraced him and kissed him* (Luke 15:20).

The father sees him first. Someone else would have probably told him to turn away. But the father was the first to see him—because he was always looking for his return.

Now look how much love the father has for this son, and how touch is a significant part of his restoration.

- The father *sees* him—no one sees him like his father.

- The father *feels* compassion—no one feels for him as much as his father.

- The father *runs to* him—his father's heart caused him to run.

- The father *embraces* him—there's no better embrace than a father for a son.

- The father *kisses* him—no one has more impact in a son's life than his father.

This story is about love, emotion, compassion, embrace, and full restoration. It is a story of a rebellious son and a loving father. It is a story of redemption. It is a story of restoration that didn't see the rags, didn't smell the filth, and didn't judge the sin.

The father Jesus spoke about here represents our heavenly Father. God is the loving Father who sees, feels, runs toward, embraces, and kisses His returning, lost children.

One Bible translation says the Father kissed him much. It wasn't just a kiss on the cheek. It was many kisses complemented by hugs and pure joy. The hug and kiss combination expressed so much love, sincerity, acceptance, and grace. All these were coming from God toward His lost son, now being restored.

What is the image of God we portray to the world? Have we personally tasted His love and compassion in this way? Have you allowed Him to hug and kiss you? Only then can you and I bear His image in a world longing for godly affection.

Soon We Can Touch

Jesus modeled the restorative effects of touch during His ministry two millennia ago. He also presented God to us as a loving

Father who touches, embraces, and kisses. He is inviting the church today into reaching out to a socially distanced society, with the mighty power of touch.

I am close to a number of people whose loved ones are fighting the coronavirus. These people's greatest pain is not being able to be by the side of those they love. One woman's parents are both infected. As I write these lines, the mother has recovered but the father has just been intubated. None of the family can be together. The recovering mother cannot be with the intubated father, nor can the children be with either of them. It is painful to know these people are meters away and yet the family cannot hold their hands, touch them and comfort them.

I know of cases here in Australia where palliative care patients (non-coronavirus infected) have chosen to suffer in pain and die at home just to have family around them, rather than being isolated on their own in hospital care. The human touch is so important.

As restrictions began to ease a bit here in Australia, I saw a neighbor of mine on the very day it was announced. He had just emerged from an eight-week self-isolation. He had no physical contact with anyone during that time. I immediately asked him if he wanted a hug. He became teary as he embraced me.

A few days later I met an elderly lady in our local park where our children play. While chatting with her I found how desperate she was for human touch. After listening to her story and her deep and meaningful needs, I asked if I could lay my hands on her and pray for her. She agreed and I placed my hands on her shoulders, prayed, and the long hug that followed brought tears of joy, smiles, and emotional healing.

You are probably not aware of this, but the need for appropriate and loving touch is so real today that not only can you pay for a body massage, you can seek out services of professional cuddlers. There are services for platonic cuddling, hand holding, and hair stroking.

There are even accredited courses in cuddle therapy. This spells out how important the human touch is.

To some, this subject may make them a bit uncomfortable, especially because of so much inappropriate touch and widespread taboos so prevalent in today's society. To make things worse, the coronavirus has added another layer of safeguarding against coming in close contact with people. Fist bumps and elbow bumps have become the new norm in replacing handshakes and hugs.

But as the church and as ministers to the needy world, we have a massive role to play in releasing the power of a touch and restoring the human touch.

As soon as we can touch, we must have a prepared awareness to engage in ministering to people in this way. It is our role to restore all that is godly in society.

Get ready to shake hands in a meaningful way. Prepare to hug and to hold people close to you. Not only the people returning to church will be in need of a loving welcome and of a meaningful touch, but also the people in the wider community. This is our ministry, yours and mine.

ONE APPLICATION

1. What will be the one personal application for you in releasing the power of touch?

2. What will be the one church application in releasing the power of touch?

CHAPTER 14

REESTABLISH SPIRITUAL FATHERHOOD

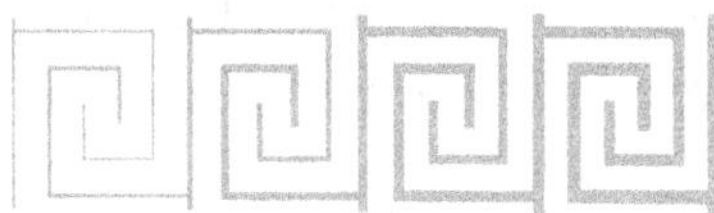

For though you have countless guides in Christ, you do not have many fathers. For I became your father in Christ Jesus through the gospel.

—1 Corinthians 4:15

The Challenges

→ *Fatherhood is generally seen as biological parenthood, not godly fatherhood.*

→ *The church is seen as an organization with an institutional view, not a relational view.*

→ *The need for a relational and parental connection has become evident during the pandemic.*

→ *The modern church has ignored the vital role of spiritual parents in the lives of believers.*

Last evening I went through one of the most humbling and honoring life experiences. I was sitting next to Dr. Bob Chapman by his hospital bedside, worshipping and praying with him while he is fighting cancer. I prayed with him in faith, laid hands on him, anointed him with oil, and we still expect the miracle of healing to happen.

Then he placed his hand on my head, and as I knelt he blessed me in an anointed prayer and passed on to me his mantle of ministry.

I lost my father when I was 16 years old, and a day never goes by that I do not miss him. When I face a challenge I naturally think that my dad would know what to do. I miss my dad. The Lord has been good to me though, He has given me other men who are fathering me. And Dr. Bob Chapman stands out as the closest to my heart.

I met Dr. Bob, as we call him, twenty-one years ago when I began my Bible training at West Australian Bible College. He was my discipleship lecturer who challenged me and everyone in the class to become true disciples of Jesus. His challenge was immersed in a strong conviction about discipleship and in his deep desire to make disciples. I had never met anyone like him before. This man was not just a teacher who had Scripture knowledge. He was dead serious about living out the discipleship lifestyle and was demanding we also step into it.

He taught me two classes on discipleship over a full year and his classes were the ones that kept my interest in studying the Word of God and living it out daily. I thrived with Dr. Bob. I took notes of almost everything he said in class, and then I reviewed them. My research and reflection papers were outstanding and I was an A+ student in his class. Later he told me I was his best student, ever. He was looking for men like me throughout his teaching and mission ministry, but very few took the call seriously.

Over the following years we met regularly, sometimes weekly, sometimes monthly, depending on our traveling schedules. He began to pour his life into me. He began to *spiritually father* me. It was more than teacher-to-apprentice discipleship. It was father-to-son, life-on-life, discipleship. He was building a long-lasting legacy through our relationship.

Dr. Bob was devoted to my journey and kept me accountable for the call of God on my life. At times he was uncomfortably harsh and direct, and at other times, gentle and understanding. He was a true father who cared for his spiritual son. He taught me how to be a father and a husband, but more than that, he *showed* me how to be a man of God. He taught me that character mattered and what I did in secret was more important than what I did in public. He confessed his sins to me and invited me to boldly do the same. He allowed me to make mistakes without rejecting or judging me, he became my spiritual mentor and my close friend, and more so, my father.

Not only did we travel the world together ministering in various nations, he also helped me write my first book, journeying with me every step. As mentioned previously, at the age of forty, I began writing *Forty Years and Forty Days*, a book written in forty days from my fortieth birthday, a chapter a day during fasting and prayer. Every morning at 4 a.m. I would write a chapter, then email it to Dr. Bob, who for forty days edited it and touched it up. He then also wrote the Foreword to the book.

I am so grateful to the Lord for sending Dr. Bob into my life, to journey with me as a father in the faith, to see how this spiritual father-son relationship can really be lived out, not just talked about in various church leadership settings.

Why am I telling you this story? Why is it important in this time? Well, we all need fatherly strength and guidance during times of uncertainty. And for many of us, the reference question echoes loudly in our ears, "What would my father do in this situation?" Sometimes we need a crisis like the coronavirus to get us thinking.

Why is this important for the church? The church has most of the time taught on spiritual fatherhood and motherhood, but has often failed to practice it. Where is this evident? It is evident in the lack of maturity and direction in both men and women during this isolation time. Christians are starving to be nurtured by spiritual parents. Christians need parental spiritual cover and mentorship.

What have we done? We preached the gospel and brought people into the life of the church as saved people, as Christians. We gave birth to them and then left them to survive on their own both in church life and in their daily life. We made pew Christians instead of disciples who become sons and daughters. Church has become a place where they go, not a family or a tribe they belong to. They have not become the church, a people who are responsible for the nurture of one another in good and bad times, in sickness and in health, until death do us part. They have not become family. They were not matured in a covenantal believer's family relationship.

Vital Lessons on Spiritual Fatherhood

A spiritual father and son relationship is one of the most powerful truths in the Bible.

The apostle Paul, even though he did not have biological sons as he was not married, took younger men under his spiritual fatherly care and training. He took Timothy as *"my true child in the faith"* (1 Timothy 1:2). Timothy's dad was not a believer (Acts 16:1). He joined Paul in his travels and became his spiritual son. Timothy grew so substantially under Paul's paternal influence that at one point Paul wrote to the Philippian church, *"For I have no one like him, who will be genuinely concerned for your welfare"* (Philippians 2:20).

In the same manner, Dr. Bob said to me that he has raised many sons but no one took the relationship to the intimate status we enjoyed.

Titus was another close disciple of Paul's, whom Paul called, *"my true child in a common faith"* (Titus 1:4). He developed immensely under Paul to the point that he even installed elders in churches (Titus 1:5).

My journey with Dr. Bob brought me some deep insights into the father-son spiritual relationship. The following are seven simple lessons I learned that will help you in your personal development and also in your church's relational development.

1. Spiritual fathers love you. This is their highest value. They make you feel safe, they accept you, and they empower you. They help you grow and break through limitations. They set a healthy atmosphere of respect and honor.

They value the relationship. This relationship grows organically and is never forced. It develops through relationship not through obligation, choices, or force. The foundation is to add value to your life.

2. Spiritual fathers are examples to follow. They carry personal integrity and have authentic life-transformation experiences. They have been through intense sifting, have learned to fight the good fight, and live what they teach. They are models we learn from.

Paul (spiritual father) reminded Timothy (spiritual son) how he modeled the Christian life:

> *You, however, have followed my teaching, my conduct, my aim in life, my faith, my patience, my love, my steadfastness, my persecutions and sufferings that happened to me...* (2 Timothy 3:10-11).

3. Spiritual fathers were sons first. The best fathers are those who were fathered. Not all would have had spiritual earthly fathers, but they would have learned to walk as sons before their Father in heaven.

They have grasped the deep and meaningful identity given to them by God, our Father, as His children. The following verse reiterates that identity twice. It first gives the name we carry, *"children of God,"* and then it seals the reality of that identity, *"and so we are."*

> *See what kind of love the Father has given to us, that we should be called **children of God; and so we are.** The reason*

why the world does not know us is that it did not know him (1 John 3:1).

4. Spiritual fathers bring freedom. The relationship dynamic is not of control—it is a relationship of freedom. They know you are your own person and you have your own walk and your own journey. What they do is enhance your relationship with God. They do not become an idol replacing your own personal walk with God, nor do you copy them in everything. They free you in your call.

5. Spiritual fathers bring spiritual covering. They battle things for you and protect you. They give you confidence to work in your area of influence. Their covering provides wisdom, interaction, and healthy warnings (1 Corinthians 4:14).

The spiritual covering also means accountability and correction. Dr. Bob used to routinely remind me of my identity, of who I really am in God. He kept bringing me back to realign with who God says I am.

Spiritual fathers do not ignore areas that need correction. They don't shame you, instead they propel you to grow. Feedback is welcome in this relationship because it brings accelerated growth. It is not a beating. It is an improvement, a step up, a fruitful enhancement of our walk with the Lord.

6. Spiritual fathers lead you into maturity. This is where the church suffers the most. Many people who are in churches today never grow up to become a mature spiritual man or woman. They remain in adolescence because they were not fathered into various stages of maturity that are necessary for growth. That is why the apostle Paul exhorted and encouraged us to walk in maturity, in a manner worthy of God.

For you know how, like a father with his children, we exhorted each one of you and encouraged you and charged you to walk in a manner worthy of God, who calls you into his own kingdom and glory (1 Thessalonians 2:11-12).

7. Spiritual fathers release an inheritance to you. They leave you their best. The things they fought for are now yours. Their ceiling is your floor. They pass it on to you as a gift. You did not earn it. It is a grace added to your journey.

They lay hands on you just as Dr. Bob did on me and release a spiritual impartation to you. The spiritual father's life leaves a mark so deep in the son's life that it becomes evident. He deposits who he is inside you so you can wake up who you are.

For this reason I remind you to fan into flame the gift of God, which is in you through the laying on of my hands (2 Timothy 1:6).

When you fan into flame the gift in you, you will have the potential to go further than they did. That's the delight of every father, to see you soar further than they did. They believe in you and that sets you up for incredible success. But before you fly with that, you need to learn to position yourself as a son and recognize this mantle of fathering on someone else's life.

Where Are the Men?

I don't know what the situation is in your church or in your part of the world, but in most of the churches I visit, I see fewer and fewer men worshipping. I see it in Australia, one of the world's most fatherless nations, and I see it throughout Asia and Europe. Where are the men?

They are busy, maybe too busy. They are at work six to seven days per week, they are playing sports on the weekends, they are pursuing their hobbies, and they are in all social spaces—bars, casinos, pubs, gyms, event centers, and recreational hubs.

They are where their desires take them, often away from their families and well away from the church.

Coronavirus now enters the scene and all of a sudden men are stuck at home, dealing with avoided issues and becoming "messed up" in real family life. They cannot hide anymore and have to deal with home issues, with the responsibilities and the leadership their family requires.

The challenge is now to "man up." Never before in history have we had this challenge and this opportunity to be the men our families need at home. And we can help men and the men in our community to put on the mantle of manhood. I love the apostle Paul's call to manhood. It is a rally just as much as it is a cry for men to be men. He said, *"Be watchful, stand firm in the faith, act like men, be strong"* (1 Corinthians 16:13).

There are competing visions out there about what a man is to be. The church of the twenty-first century has a massive, unaddressed problem. The devil knows that if he takes down the men, he destroys the family—and as such, society.

The call of the apostle is a call to bravery, of courage and responsibility in face of danger and frightening circumstances. The call is to put aside any fear that inhibits men to follow Christ and to get on with it regardless of the emotion. It challenges men to fear God above anything else and push on in life no matter what. In its true sense, it is a call to responsible manhood.

Before we can reestablish spiritual fatherhood, we need to restore men to their rightful calling. The coronavirus exposed this need more so than ever. They are not where God has placed them. They try to fit into family life rather than belonging to it and leading it. Our men need to be restored to their manhood calling.

They need to be restored to being responsible, providing for their family, offering direction and leadership, and to being true husbands and fathers. Only then can they come up higher to spiritual fatherhood.

Where Are the Spiritual Fathers?

The church is lacking spiritual fathers and every crisis reveals what we are missing. They are rare because this was never emphasized and modeled as a way of life, only taught as a biblical principle.

Many Christians would love the idea of being spiritual fathers and mothers and they see the need in the church. What they are missing is a practical model. They have not walked as sons and daughters, so how can they father and mother others?

The church needs to return to a family dynamic of understanding itself, rather than an organization. The church functions should first be family-based functions. The emphasis should be on family identity in Christ, our identity in the Christian family. I am talking about sons, daughters, mothers, fathers, brothers, and sisters.

Embracing a family dynamic in the church will nurture the functions to develop. As people recognize their identity in God as their Father, in Christ as their big Brother, and in one another as brothers and sisters, they will begin to step into the roles they have in the church family. And as they journey, they mature in their roles so they become mothers and fathers.

Our spiritual fathers and mothers are already in our churches. They simply have not stepped up to that call. They haven't fully matured yet. They haven't been asked to take on the roles. And even if they were asked, they haven't had the skills to do it.

During the pandemic, people have turned to close family for help, advice, and guidance. If the church was a close family, then no Christian would feel isolated. No Christian would be anxious, lonely, or afraid. No Christian would fall by the wayside. No young people would be disillusioned. Everyone would have the support of the church family.

Challenges will come again. Crises will come again. The coronavirus situation has taught us that we haven't formed church family too well. And the missing piece is the paternal aspect. Spiritual fatherhood was poorly done. It's time for realignment.

ONE APPLICATION

1. What is the one aspect you will jump on and practice in spiritual parenting?

2. What is the one aspect you will implement in your church for spiritual parenting?

CHAPTER 15

RETHINK ESCHATOLOGY

He said to them, "It is not for you to know times or seasons that the Father has fixed by his own authority."

—Acts 1:7

The Challenges

→ *The church has an unbalanced grip on Eschatology, either ignoring it or going too deep into it.*

→ *Unfiltered Eschatology is one of Christianity's biggest challenges.*

→ *Many in the church believe the coronavirus era leads to the end of the world.*

→ *Church leaders are tempted to portray strong views toward the end time.*

In January 1999, when I enrolled in the Graduate Diploma of Christian Ministry at West Australian Bible College, I was searching for a new Bible I could buy to aid my studies. Visiting my local Bible store I was drawn to a Spirit-Filled New King James Bible.

I loved it because it had notes at the beginning, loads of notes at the end, and plenty of studies throughout it. Then I discovered it had a study on the second coming of the Lord, and that intrigued me.

I read the study and while going through it I felt confused and quite irritated by what I was reading. There were twelve accepted views on the second coming, all strongly backed up with Scriptures. It shook me. I have heard of pre-tribulation, mid-tribulation, and post-tribulation views of Jesus' second return, but now twelve "accepted" views?

Then to make matters even more confusing, in our study of Eschatology (which simply means study of end things) at Bible college, we were challenged to prove that not all of Matthew 24 was an end-time prophecy but something already fulfilled in the period of the early church with the fall of Jerusalem, with only a small part still to happen. That caused a real stir in me as I had never considered it. And you know what, most of Matthew 24 can be traced to events that took place in that era.

During that time in my life I was also working in the information technology field for the federal government at the Australian Bureau of Statistics. As we were preparing for Y2K (transition to year 2000), I realized that the world was advancing at such a fast pace and the end could be quite near.

In my church life experience I noticed that some aspects of the end of the world were preached but rarely taught, studied, or debated as such. The book of Revelation was avoided as it seemed too overwhelming and the prophecies of the major and minor prophets were not studied in depth. As such, most Christians chased teachings on the end things at conferences, seminars, and lately online, and many bought and studied endless numbers of books on the subject. For some believers, this remains an intriguing and nagging subject that is yet to somehow mature in their understanding.

It is, however, Christianity's most lucrative subject when it comes to selling books or recordings. That is frightening. No other Christian book topic gets more sales than those focusing on the end times. Check your library and see where you stand.

Is the church doing eschatology justice? Well, based on what is currently going on in the virtual space with Christians, I would say, no. The current pandemic has raised the possibility of this time being the end of the world. Combine this with the lockdown that has given people so much idle time and access to the web in an unprecedented way, anyone and everyone can now expose their views; and strangely enough, there's an audience ready to listen and engage.

Prophets, true and false, have come out of the closet giving their words, views, and predictions about the end times, and thousands upon thousands are feeding on their aligned or distorted explanations. Unfiltered content fills the Internet space and rousingly enters the ears and hearts of many believers, unbalancing their outlook toward the end times. And what is even more frightening is that most people do not care whether the views exposed are biblical or not. They never tax the preacher or the prophet anymore. It is accepted more as entertainment than sound teaching.

I have never received so many prophecies from my circle of people I know worldwide. Never before have people shared with me so many videos pointing to the end of the world during this pandemic or soon after. Christianity is taken on a rollercoaster ride again, just like it was in every other generation before us, and most of us are tempted to be drawn yet again into it.

What Do We Learn from History?

History teaches us that even the early church was preparing for the second coming of the Lord. Since then, every generation thought the same.

When we look only at the last century, we will be amazed how many times Christians believed the world would end. Here's a brief glimpse:

- World War I
- Spanish Flu, 1918 (over 50 million died)
- Russian Revolution and Communism
- Economic Depression
- Rise of Dictatorship
- World War II
- The Holocaust
- Nuclear Age
- Cold War
- Technology Age
- Global Warming (later redefined as Climate Change)
- Year 2000
- September 11
- GFC (Global Financial Crisis)
- And now, COVID-19

In every generation there were a number of events that triggered a thought pattern of a possible end of the world. And each passed us by. Did they do any good? I believe they did. They created a sense of urgency for Christians to ensure their relationship with Christ was genuine, real, and prioritized—and also brought others into the faith. Did these crises do any damage? I believe some damage, yes. Those who watched Christians be carried away with it became more disillusioned with Christianity.

If you do a simple search on Christians who predicted the second coming of Christ in their time, you will come across an entire Wikipedia page full of entries about people who thought the world was near its final day.

I was born in 1972, and even in my short time here on earth I experienced some close encounters with end-time possibilities. As you know by now, I was born in communist Romania, and many thought our dictator, Ceausescu, was the antichrist (or more so, the USSR leader, Gorbachev), then the Catholic Pope, later on Barak Obama, and now Bill Gates.

In the 1970s when Christians heard about the electronic chip being so small and carrying so much data, they believed it was the sign of the beast that was to be inserted in the human hand or forehead. Later in the '80s it was the barcode that was simply read by the scanner, and many wouldn't purchase products with barcodes on them. The late 1990s was preparation for Year 2000, also known as Y2K, and so much was written and prophesied about this "end-time." Then the World Trade Center twin towers were attacked and collapsed in New York that signaled another possible finale, not to mention the GFC. Fast forward to 2020, and with the COVID-19 attached to the launching of the 5G, there was another perfect end-of-the-world story.

Now, take all of that and combine it with two major events of recent history: 1) world globalization, characterized by unprecedented technology advancements; and 2) the return of the nation of Israel to its promised land, and things begin to line up. Saying, "We live in the end times" has been an accepted Christian cliché for this period of history.

You may or may not be aware, but there is a Rapture Index website that studies the activities that could act as precursors to the rapture. Christians have been fascinated by end-time stories for a long time. The popularity of the *Left Behind* book series signaled how obsessed we can become with the end of the world scenario.

Why do we tend to embrace this eschatology even though history tells us different? For some it's because they want the end to be in their lifetime, they want to escape death. Yes, the fear of dying is real for many Christians. For others it's because they can see it happening, there is enough evidence for the rational mind to see it happening in this time. The technology gives them enough evidence for the antichrist to come and control the world. Watching the political development of Israel, China, Russia, and the US brings some possible alignment with Scriptures for others.

What Do Pastors See in Current Events?

Lifeway Research conducted a survey[1] study on 1,000 pastors from evangelical and historically black denominations in the USA, between January 24 and February 11, 2020, a few weeks before COVID-19 was widely spread. The findings may surprise you. This is not a worldwide view of all pastors, but it does give a good glimpse based on the sample studied. The entire study is found at the link cited in the chapter endnote. Portions of the survey follow:

- At least 3 in 4 pastors agree Jesus was referring to current events including the rise of false prophets and false teachings (83%), the love of many believers growing cold (81%), traditional morals becoming less accepted (79%), wars and national conflicts (78%), earthquakes and other natural disasters (76%), and people abandoning their Christian faith (75%).

- Clear majorities also see famines (70%) and anti-Semitism toward Jewish people worldwide (63%) as signs of Jesus' return.

- Around 1 in 10 pastors (11%) say they don't consider any of these part of the birth pains to which Jesus was referring.

- More than half of pastors (56%) expect Jesus to return in their lifetime.

- While most say they expect Jesus to return while they're still alive, as many pastors say they're not sure (24%) as say they strongly agree (25%). Three in 10 somewhat agree (31%), while 20% disagree, including 6% who strongly disagree.

- Among those more likely to disagree Jesus will return during their lifetime are pastors ages 18 to 44 (27%) and pastors of churches with 250 or more in attendance (28%).

- Most pastors also believe it is important to study and teach on biblical prophecies and eschatology.

- Around 3 in 5 say it is important to preach on end times prophecies in the book of Revelation (60%) and the Old Testament (60%), as well as spend time personally studying eschatology (57%).

- A quarter of pastors (24%) speak to their congregations about end times prophecies at least once a month. Close to half (48%) say they do so several times a year.

- Around 1 in 10 pastors say they talk about it with their church about once a year (11%). The same number (11%) say they do so rarely. Few say they never speak to their congregation about those prophecies (3%).

Personally, I asked a number of mature leaders and pastors in Australia about the possibility of the end of the world, and very few agreed with the view of this study.

Some told me there are many prophetic words the Lord gave them, which are yet to be fulfilled in their lifetime. Others emphasized how much the Lord wants people to be saved and that is why the world will go on. One pointed me to the fact that the ancient temple in Jerusalem had to be rebuilt first and many ignore this simple characteristic. He also said that we should look more at Israel than to disease, because there are more prophecies about the land of Israel and its people than about the tribulations and signs in the world. (For more information about this aspect, see the full article at the LifeWay link.)

If the events of the coronavirus cause concern, it should bring people to Jesus. If this could be the sign of things to come, then the church should be encouraged to get ready and be ready.

What Do We *Learn* from Jesus?

Did Jesus speak about the end times? Yes, He did. However, it was not a priority topic for Him. In fact it was twelfth on the list of major topics He spoke about. What was the number one subject, you may ask? No, it wasn't money. It was God! He mentioned and spoke about God more than any other topic. And He did talk about the end days, but not as the utmost priority.

What did Jesus say about the end times? He simply said to stay awake!

*"But concerning that day or that hour, no one knows, not even the angels in heaven, nor the Son, but only the Father. Be on guard, **keep awake**. For you do not know when the time will come. It is like a man going on a journey, when he leaves home and puts his servants in charge, each with his work, and commands the doorkeeper to stay awake. Therefore **stay awake**—for you do not know when the master of the house will come, in the evening, or at midnight, or when the rooster crows, or in the morning—lest he come*

*suddenly and find you asleep. And what I say to you I say to all: **Stay awake**"* (Mark 13:32-37).

Jesus gives us a couple of vital lessons we cannot ignore:

1. No one knows when Jesus will return. Not even Jesus Himself knows when He will return, only the Father. It is concealed. Why do we get concerned with pinpointing the return of Christ when He specifically told us that no one knows. It may be because, just as the first man and woman, Adam and Eve, we want to eat of the fruit of knowledge in regard to His return. Can we accept this?

2. Be on guard, keep awake. This is our part. Be alert. Be ready. Look. Be vigilant. Be on watch. Be sober. Stay awake. The events of today and similar events of history could well be interpreted as signs of the end. But this is debatable and even the Gospel narratives of Matthew 24 and Mark 13 can be interpreted as non-end-time prophecies. So, we keep vigilant and awake—we are on watch in every generation.

What Were Jesus' *Instructions* Before Ascending to the Father?

It is surprisingly remarkable how little the church looks at the first part of Jesus' final words before ascending to the Father, in the first chapter of the book of Acts. It seems there is such a familiarity with verse 8 and great ignorance toward verse 7 where Jesus begins His speech.

So when they had come together, they asked him, "Lord, will you at this time restore the kingdom to Israel?" He said to them, "It is not for you to know times or seasons that the Father has fixed by his own authority. But you will receive power when the Holy Spirit has come upon you, and you will

*be my witnesses in Jerusalem and in all Judea and Samaria,
and to the end of the earth"* (Acts 1:6-8).

The disciples, having seen the risen Lord and still coming to grips with believing it, asked Him about the time of the kingdom restoration. This question was a reference to end times. His answer is astonishing! *"It's not for you to know..."* In essence He was saying, STOP the inquiry. Don't be concerned with the times and the seasons. These are set, in fact they are fixed by the Father by His own authority. Why do you want to know when it is not for you to know?

And He continues, in essence and emphatically saying to His disciples: What am I calling you to do? I want you to receive power and be My witnesses here and then going everywhere with the gospel. Just do these two things, receive power and be My witnesses. This is your part, this is your call, this is what I want you to focus on. Don't get sidetracked into working out times and seasons. It is futile. It is a waste of time and energy. Get busy with what the kingdom is about—power and witnessing.

These were Jesus' instructions:

1. Wait for the Promised Gift of the Holy Spirit. Do not leave Jerusalem (yet).

2. Be baptized with the Holy Spirit.

3. It's not for you to know the times or seasons.

4. These are fixed by God so trust Him and His authority.

5. You receive power!

6. You be My witnesses!

7. This is a worldwide commission!

Has this directive changed? No. Nothing has changed since then. We are simply to receive the Holy Spirit, not get entangled with end-time rhetoric; and trusting God for this, tap into the Spirit's power and be His witnesses at home and everywhere.

Can you imagine where the church would be today if it simply obeyed His command? Rather than this simplicity, the church gets carried away and entangled in a wide array of end-time stories that consume it. Christians can easily chase end-time prophets with doom and gloom prophetic words who create addictions and ongoing dependency or more. And before we know it we are carried away and become either strongly opinionated or worse, mystical in our eschatology.

Apostle Peter's Directive

Assuming that we are seeing end-time signs, our task as Christians is not to panic or run for the hills or start stockpiling food and weapons adopting a fortress mentality. What should we do?

Apostle Peter gives us an important directive:

> *But the day of the Lord will come like a thief, and then the heavens will pass away with a roar, and the heavenly bodies will be burned up and dissolved, and the earth and the works that are done on it will be exposed. Since all these things are thus to be dissolved, **what sort of people ought you to be in lives of holiness and godliness, waiting for and hastening the coming of the day of God**, because of which the heavens will be set on fire and dissolved, and the heavenly bodies will melt as they burn!* (2 Peter 3:10-12)

Look at the simplicity of Peter's message. End-time Christians are to practice holiness and do good everywhere to everyone. In other terms, they are to do the works of God *"while it is day"* (John 9:4). Why? Because Jesus can return anytime.

The apostle Peter reaffirmed the words of the Lord Jesus who promised to return like a thief in the night (Matthew 24:42-44; Revelation 3:3, 16:15). And then the finale begins with a catastrophic ending.

Throughout history the teachings on these end times have widely varied, but what is important is this—Jesus will return, God will judge sin, and the earth will be destroyed by fire.

When will this happen is not known. He did not indicate when, only what will happen. It's easy to get carried away and read into the current events as this is it.

If you believe this is the end of the world, prove it by the life you live. Show me the love, surrender, service, and the commitment in doing the kingdom work like never before. Show me no restraint in sharing the gospel and desiring in an all-consuming way the salvation of everyone you meet. Forget theories, forget views, forget perspectives, forget writings or speeches on the subject—show me you live out what you believe. And if you cannot, rethink your stance.

Rethinking Eschatology in a Healthy Way

Eschatology is important and it matters. Even though this is not as vital as understanding the person and work of Christ, it is still critical for our healthy outlook to the future and for a holistic understanding of the work of God.

Some churches keep away from eschatology, avoiding a serious study of it because of the many complexities and differing views. At the other end of the spectrum are churches and individuals who have become obsessed with Jesus' return, either offering a date or treating every event as biblical prophecy.

The current coronavirus situation leads the church back to rethink its view of the end things because its people have questions. They are looking for answers and often end up looking in the wrong places and soon adhere to skewed views. This is a dangerous time for the church. It is a divisive subject and the weak and vulnerable in the Word are at risk.

What is then a healthy way to approach eschatology during this period? What direction can we give people? What can we teach them about end times? The following are some healthy points to remember:

1. Jesus is coming back.

The Bible promises a literal return of Jesus Christ. This is the greatest part of the end times—Jesus returns.

> *And just as it is appointed for man to die once, and after that comes judgment, so Christ, having been offered once to bear the sins of many, will appear a second time, not to deal with sin but to save those who are eagerly waiting for him* (Hebrews 9:27-28).

Jesus' ascension was before witnesses who not only saw Him lifted up, they also saw and heard the two angels reaffirming His second return—just as physical as His first.

> *And when he had said these things, as they were looking on, he was lifted up, and a cloud took him out of their sight. And while they were gazing into heaven as he went, behold, two men stood by them in white robes, and said, "Men of Galilee, why do you stand looking into heaven? This Jesus, who was taken up from you into heaven, will come in the same way as you saw him go into heaven"* (Acts 1:9-11).

2. No one knows when Jesus returns.

Simply put, no one knows when Jesus will come back—not even Himself, only Father God knows.

> *But concerning that day and hour no one knows, not even the angels of heaven, nor the Son, but the Father only* (Matthew 24:36)

Shortly afterward in verse 42, Jesus tells us to stay awake, to be ready. Why do people want to know when? It is because they want to manipulate the situation in their favor. They don't want to stay awake, they don't want to be ready. They want to control their lives leading toward Jesus' second coming. They don't realize that death may be a few breaths away and for them, Jesus would have already come.

You will probably argue that Jesus also gave us plenty of signs preceding His return, so we can get a seasonal indication. True, He did. But if Jesus told us that no one knows, why do people then have this insatiable desire to know? Why do people want to predict something God says we will never know? Why can't we just simply leave it there?

Jesus commanded us to prepare and be ready for His second return. If this event can happen anytime in the future, it could happen anytime—even today.

3. Christians are to look forward to His return.

As Christians we should be eagerly waiting for Jesus' return. This is our blessed hope that He is coming back for us, to take us with Him in glory. This is the complete gospel. It is part of our complete Christian storyline.

The apostle Paul reminded Timothy and us of our blessed future.

For the grace of God has appeared, bringing salvation for all people, training us to renounce ungodliness and worldly passions, and to live self-controlled, upright, and godly lives in the present age, waiting for our blessed hope, the appearing of the glory of our great God and Savior Jesus Christ, who gave himself for us to redeem us from all lawlessness and to purify for himself a people for his own possession who are zealous for good works (Titus 2:11-14).

This world is not our home. We are here temporarily. We are going to be with the Lord for eternity. We are on earth, but we are not of earth. We are citizens of heaven (Philippians 3:20). We are reborn of above and we're going home, be it through the passage of death or through rapture if we're alive at His second coming.

Our future is assured. There is no need to predict it. Jesus will restore all things to Himself. Evil's only triumph is on this side of eternity. The suffering and trials of our current age will not last forever. Christ's righteousness and goodness will win in the end.

If Christians do not look forward to His return, it is because they fear the coming judgment. The world should be afraid of His judgment, absolutely—but not the followers of Jesus. The eternal division is real, eternal life with God or eternal perishing. Heaven is real and so is hell. The story does not end well for everyone.

As Christians our focus should be on eternity. We should have an unquenchable zeal and passion to worship God, to follow Him, and to share His truth with everyone. The thought of last things should not bring us fear, but rather assured joy.

4. Christians are to share eschatology in a healthy way.

Most people in the world do not want to think about what happens after death, except when they are close to dying. The devil uses every means to lure them into ignoring eternity. Satan is the father of lies who keeps people bound in the lie that it is all about this life (John 8:44).

As Christians we have a major role to play in offering people the real godly perspective. The fear of death is real to everyone and we have hope beyond the grave. We have the opportunity and the means to bring spiritual truth to this taboo subject. The coronavirus situation has provided for us an open door into the subject. We have the responsibility to talk about eschatology to those we witness to and later disciple.

Even people in our churches are asking for direction, especially in this time of uncertainty. They should hear our healthy perspective before they consider going anywhere else. And our views don't need to be strongly skewed toward one school of thought. Why? We change. Do you remember how you viewed eschatology twenty years ago? It was probably different from how you view it today. Our salvation doesn't hang on the eschatological interpretation we have at a certain point on our Christian faith journey. Most views have ultimately the same belief—Jesus is returning and judgment is coming. This is what should be the most essential ingredient of our story and the story we share with others. It is keeping the main thing, the main thing.

Apostle Paul did not shrink from declaring to the elders of Ephesus the *whole counsel of God* (Acts 20:27). If we are not teaching it, who will? This is why so many church people keep looking elsewhere. We haven't simplified it for them to offer sound doctrinal clarity.

In this season as we reflect on our eschatology narrative, can I invite you to rethink it in light of what I stirred in this chapter and see where the Spirit leads you to bring stability and hope for others. They are asking for your leadership, not your views. They need healthy navigation, not heavier content. And the Lord positioned you to lead them in this season. Rise above the current situation and lead.

ONE APPLICATION

1. What is the one shift you will make in your personal life regarding eschatology?

2. What is the one shift you can apply in your church ministry regarding eschatology?

Endnote

1. Aaron Earls, "Vast Majority of Pastors See Signs of End Times in Current Events," April 7, 2020; https://lifewayresearch.com/2020/04/07/vast-majority-of-pastors-see-signs-of-end-times-in-current-events/; accessed August 22, 2020.

REFOCUS ON THE KINGDOM

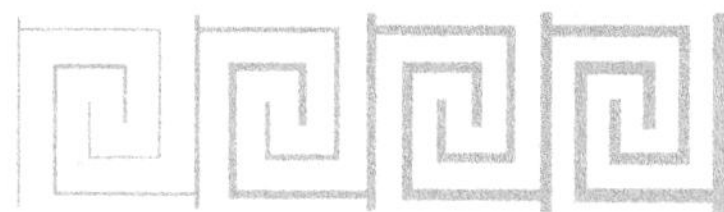

For the kingdom of God does not consist in talk but in power.

—1 Corinthians 4:20

The Challenges

→ *The church's priorities are exposed in crisis and need to be questioned.*

→ *The pandemic challenges the church to refocus on the importance of the kingdom of God.*

→ *The church talks of the kingdom but does not manifest the kingdom.*

→ *The challenge behind the challenge is our identity in the kingdom.*

One of the proudest moments of my life as a father was when my four-year-old daughter, Evangeline, stood up in church and recited the Lord's Prayer memorized. Almost every night we prayed it together; and although she may not understand it all, she has it ingrained in her.

While she was praying it, I thought about the fact that most Christians know it off by heart, pray it, and yet they don't really mean it. Do they really want God's name to be praised above all else (Matthew 6:9)? Do they truly ask for God's kingdom and His will do be done on earth as it is in heaven (Matthew 6:10)? Do they really understand His kingdom?

For a moment, there and then, time stood still for me. While enjoying her prayer in front of the church, the Spirit stirred me and challenged me on how real is God's kingdom for me and my church.

As a church leader, I immediately asked myself, *How well have I communicated the kingdom of God to the church I lead. Do I see it manifested in my everyday? Do I see the folk I lead running with it on a daily basis? Have I lost my focus? Where, in terms of priorities, is God's kingdom?*

Fast forward a couple of years and the coronavirus hits the world. While there's concern and worry all around, the Lord challenged me with these nagging questions, "Are you prioritizing My kingdom? Is the kingdom of God what you focus on, or the problem? Does the coronavirus change anything for you in terms of your priorities? What did Jesus say when the temptation is to worry about tomorrow? He said to seek His kingdom and righteousness first and all else will taken care of (Matthew 6:33). Is this an opportunity to put in practice this reality of kingdom life?"

Life begins at age forty, they say. They were right, you know. This restart may not happen exactly at forty but somewhere in that vicinity. Until my early forties, I had more answers than questions. Sad, I know. My level of awareness both spiritually and emotionally was so low that I did not know there was a scale. I had no real sense of that reality. Ignorance.

But the Lord's patience hasn't run dry. His work in me was just beginning. So He triggered something in recent years, a deeper sense of awareness, a deeper sense of inquiry and zillions of questions running non-stop through my head and my spirit. This awareness brings with it a hunger for clarity that takes me often to a sharper focus on spiritual subjects on my spiritual journey. And the kingdom of God is one such topic.

Kingdom Focus Means Kingdom Clarity

If we were to ask most churches where their focus is, we would find it to be linked to some sort of ministry, project, or program. Church leaders would tell us they are focused on reaching the lost in their community, or on their youth, or on the Sunday services, or on a specific project they are working on. All this seems to be part of the greater call of God on their ministry, and in some way it is. But how many of them truly focus on these aspects through the lenses of the kingdom of God?

Do you know that you only get what you focus on, in exclusion of everything else? What you focus on magnifies, and what you don't ceases to exist. If your focus is not on the kingdom of God, for you it has very little significance. But if this is your primary focus, then this kingdom mystery is not only revealed to you, it becomes your primary practice. And only when we focus on God's kingdom do we get a real sense of our identity in the context of it.

You see, all is well until we hit a brick wall, a coronavirus hurdle that challenges us to go deeper, to go further, to push through and overcome it. Unless we have some deep and meaningful understanding of our place in the overall work of God, we can be easily disillusioned or even taken down. Behind the challenge of running the church, there are deeper challenges. And one of the deepest challenges revealed by the pandemic is how we identify with the kingdom of God.

Before we can identify with it, we need to understand what it is, how it works and what role do we play in it. Let me offer you some clarity on God's kingdom.

1. God's kingdom is not from here.

God's kingdom is a heavenly kingdom manifested on earth. It is from above. It is vital to understand this because it works on heavenly terms, not earthly ones. If we look at it from our earthly perspective, we reduce it to our worldly limitations. It is not of this world—that's what Jesus told Pilate. Let's recall the account:

> *So Pilate entered his headquarters again and called Jesus and said to him, "Are you the King of the Jews?" Jesus answered, "Do you say this of your own accord, or did others say it to you about me?" Pilate answered, "Am I a Jew? Your own nation and the chief priests have delivered you over to me. What have you done?" Jesus answered, "My kingdom is not of this world. If my kingdom were of this world, my servants would have been fighting, that I might not be delivered over to the Jews. But my kingdom is not from the world." Then Pilate said to him, "So you are a king?" Jesus answered, "You say that I am a king. For this purpose I was born and for this purpose I have come into the world—to bear witness to the truth. Everyone who is of the truth listens to my voice"* (John 18:33-37).

When Jesus described God's kingdom, He revealed to us a few powerful insights. His kingdom is not from here, it is from heaven. His kingdom does not operate in earthly forms, there is another heavenly way of winning people over to this kingdom. His kingdom was for Him, and belonged to Him; He was born for it and will lead it in truth. His ministry was heavenly even though it was manifested on earth.

We act as if our ministry is earthly. We act as if everything is about us—our church, our ministry, our city, and our country. It seems that way but it isn't. Our identity should not be given by our ministry or by what we do. Our identity must be deeply rooted into who King Jesus says we are. And this is how He sees us.

I do not ask that you take them out of the world, but that you keep them from the evil one. They are not of the world, just as I am not of the world. Sanctify them in the truth; your word is truth. As you sent me into the world, so I have sent them into the world (John 17:15-18).

There's powerful truth here about the identity we inherit in Christ that we should not ignore nor overlook:

- We are in the world and we are to live in the world (John 17:15).

- We are protected from the devil (John 17:15).

- But we are not of the world—just like Jesus isn't, because we are born of Christ, born of above, so we do not belong here (John17:16).

- We are sanctified by God's truth (John 17:17).

- We are sent into the world—just like Jesus, we go into the world from our non-earthly identity (John 17:18).

I believe we are quite comfortable with the first part of Jesus not being of this world. The provoking thought is about our heavenly identity. Do we believe we are not of this world anymore? Because if we do, this changes everything. We are on earth, but not of the earth. This means nothing that goes on in this world unsettles us. We are here on a mission, just like Jesus, to testify of the truth. For this purpose we are born of above—to represent our new identity as kingdom people and to extend God's kingdom citizenship to others.

2. The kingdom of God is here.

The first sermon preached by Jesus and recorded by the Gospel writers is the gospel of the kingdom. This is before Jesus made any disciples:

> *Now after John was arrested, **Jesus came into Galilee, proclaiming the gospel** of God, and saying, "The time is fulfilled, and **the kingdom of God is at hand;** repent and believe in the gospel"* (Mark 1:14-15).

Jesus' introduction to His earthly ministry tells us He had a kingdom focus from the start. The wait is over, the prophecies are fulfilling and the kingdom of God is at hand—within reach, ready to be entered into by anyone who repents and believes. It is now here and accessible to anyone. The wait is over. There is no need to wait for this life to end to then enter God's kingdom. It has become reachable and is readily available.

There is an aspect of the kingdom that is yet to happen in the eternal heavenly realm, but we must be aware of the reality that it has already begun. The new era of the kingdom began with King Jesus. He came to restore all things to God, to restore the reign of God in God's creation.

We can live in the kingdom realm, here and now. This is a mystery that not all Christians have yet embraced. Remember when the disciples asked Jesus why He spoke in parables about God's kingdom? Let me remind you what He said:

> *And he answered them, "To you it has been given to know the secrets of the kingdom of heaven, but to them it has not been given"* (Matthew 13:11).

God reveals secrets about the kingdom of heaven to His disciples. And He wants us to come to grips in understanding these revelations. They have been *given* to us. These mysteries are for us, here and now to understand and live in the kingdom dimension.

Why didn't Jesus just ask them to receive the gospel of salvation. He gives a kingdom gospel far deeper than the salvation gospel. The salvation gospel deals with our past, and we need to be saved from our past life full of sin. But what are we to be saved onto?

"Good works," you may say. But it's deeper than that. You are to be saved to a kingdom reality. You are to make Jesus Christ the King of your life, not only the Savior of your life. A kingdom gospel makes Jesus Christ the King and Lord of your life, not just your Savior who died for you.

Jesus identified with the kingdom gospel. When He revealed His ministry to the crowds, He did not shy away from giving them this spiritual truth:

But he said to them, "I must preach the good news of the kingdom of God to the other towns as well; for I was sent for this purpose" (Luke 4:43).

Jesus could have said His purpose was to preach the good news of salvation. That's what most of us would say. Unfortunately that's what we do say. Jesus identified with the *"good news of the kingdom of God."* This is radically deeper and more meaningful. Jesus shows His focus in His mission.

Notice He says, He *"was sent for this purpose."* In John 18:37 in front of Pilate Jesus says, *"For this purpose I was born."* Yes, He was *born* for this, but deeper still, He was *sent* for this. The restoration of God's kingdom was His mission. Nothing would take Him from His assignment. His made up His mind and His laser-focus vision was in fulfilling His assignment. I love Luke's record of Jesus' stubbornness to remain focused on His mission:

When the days drew near for him to be taken up, he set his face to go to Jerusalem (Luke 9:51).

Determinedly, resolutely, steadfastly, He intently set His face to go to Jerusalem, even though He knew death awaited Him. He identified with the kingdom and wants us to have a life that resembles His. Our ministry should display a solid focus on God's kingdom. Our faces as believers should be toward God's kingdom. People should be taught to set their faces on God's kingdom.

3. God's kingdom is within you.

Jesus was asked by the Pharisees where was God's kingdom. His answer gives away another important secret of His kingdom.

> *Being asked by the Pharisees when the kingdom of God would come, he answered them, "The kingdom of God is not coming in ways that can be observed, nor will they say, 'Look, here it is!' or 'There!' for behold, the kingdom of God is in the midst of you"* (Luke 17:20-21).

You will not see the kingdom if you're trying to observe it. It doesn't come by observation. If you are trying to see it, you will not (John 3:3). Again, it's much deeper than that. It is among you, in the midst of you, better yet, it is *within* you.

This kingdom is not a political kingdom. It is a spiritual kingdom that only becomes real when Christ becomes someone's King. This happens internally, it is an inside-out work. It happens when someone changes kings. Apostle Paul got it. He said in Colossians 1:13, *"He has delivered us from the domain of darkness and transferred us to the kingdom of his beloved Son."*

If the kingdom of God is real inside us, it cannot be shaken by anything. We have been delivered from the dark kingdoms. We have a new kingdom, Jesus' kingdom.

Look at Nicodemus' journey of discovering God's kingdom for himself:

> *Now there was a man of the Pharisees named Nicodemus, a ruler of the Jews. This man came to Jesus by night and said to him, "Rabbi, we know that you are a teacher come from God, for no one can do these signs that you do unless God is with him." Jesus answered him, "Truly, truly, I say to you, **unless one is born again he cannot see the kingdom of God.**" Nicodemus said to him, "How can a man*

*be born when he is old? Can he enter a second time into his mother's womb and be born?" Jesus answered, "Truly, truly, I say to you, **unless one is born of water and the Spirit, he cannot enter the kingdom of God.** That which is born of the flesh is flesh, and that which is born of the Spirit is spirit"* (John 3:1-6).

Jesus tells Nicodemus he needs to be born again to *see* the kingdom. His new birth has to be in the kingdom, not just into salvation. Everyone loves Jesus as Savior, but what about as King and Lord of their lives.

And then Jesus challenges Nicodemus further to not just see it but to *enter* it. The entrance into the kingdom is the birth of water and of the Spirit, not just of water. Water baptism and Spirit filling bring the reality of the kingdom of God. Otherwise we operate in the flesh, even as Christians. Jesus gives the secret to kingdom entrance—a Spirit rebirth.

The Word of God washes and cleanses us (Ephesians 5:26). The more Word we have in our life, the more we are led by the Spirit of God, and gradually Jesus is embodied in us. You've heard God's Word, you read it, you meditated on it, you believed it, and now you have to let it manifest in you, become flesh in you. As apostle Paul put it, *"Let the word of Christ dwell in you richly..."* (Colossians 3:16).

You enter into the dimension of the kingdom of God when the Word of God is alive, enfleshed and embodied in you. You have to see this aspect first.

You enter into the full dimension of the kingdom of God when you operate in the Spirit's realm. The kingdom of God is spiritual. You don't engage in it in the flesh. You don't fight in the flesh. You win every battle in the Spirit. The battle is spiritual and it is *"against the rulers, against the authorities, against the cosmic powers over this present darkness, against the spiritual forces of evil in the heavenly places"* (Ephesians 6:12). You cannot fight these in the flesh.

This truth is vital for our period of uncertainty. Is the coronavirus a spiritual battle? Yes it is even though it is manifested in the earthly realm. How do we claim victory? In the spiritual realm with the weapons of the Spirit. That's how things work in the kingdom.

We bring it all back to God. We bring this and every situation to the reign of God. We bring every person to the lordship and kingship of God, one by one. Nothing changes. We want God's dominion in every heart.

God's Kingdom *Manifests* with Power

There is a test for us to undertake if we want to know where we stand when it comes to focusing on the kingdom of God and living in it. The test is in proving it with power. Apostle Paul said, *"For the kingdom of God does not consist in talk but in power"* (1 Corinthians 4:20).

There has been enough talk about the kingdom. It's time for manifestation. Believers have heard far too many words and seen very little power. Can we demonstrate God's kingdom at work in us and through us?

Jesus said His kingdom ministry can be tested through the signs and miracles He was performing. He said to the Pharisees who were accusing Him of using the prince of demons to cast out demons, *"But if it is by the Spirit of God that I cast out demons, then the kingdom of God has come upon you"* (Matthew 12:28). Jesus was giving them proof of the reality of the kingdom. Only something stronger can drive out the demons in a person. Therefore if someone is freed from demonic powers, this proves the kingdom of God, which is stronger, is at work.

Apostle Paul also depended on the Spirit's power for his ministry. We can get by without it, and many do. The Scripture I am about to refresh in your mind right now is one of the most humbling, and has affected my ministry in recent years:

> *And I, when I came to you, brothers, did not come proclaiming to you the testimony of God with lofty speech or wisdom. For I decided to know nothing among you except Jesus Christ and him crucified. And I was with you in weakness and in fear and much trembling, and my speech and my message were not in plausible words of wisdom, but in demonstration of the Spirit and of power, so that your faith might not rest in the wisdom of men but in the power of God* (1 Corinthians 2:1-5).

Look at Paul's life in the kingdom realm! It is fully dependent on Christ, His Spirit, and God. His ministry was not about his eloquence of speech nor his impressing wisdom. Paul even made a conscious decision not to show off in any way. He decided to forget his wisdom and his capacity to teach. All Paul wanted to talk about was the kingdom of God, whose King, Jesus Christ, was crucified. That was the center of his message, the message of the King. And Paul expected the power contained in that message to have the greatest impact.

In order to prove the power of the message of Christ, Paul's words were purposely weak allowing himself to flow in the Spirit to demonstrate God's power. The reason for this was to connect everyone to the power of God and not to someone's ministry or personality. Paul wanted those who heard him to become people of the kingdom who manifest its power.

All around us desperate people are waiting for God's power to be manifested, and you and I carry it. I want to cry out, "Enough words!" Maybe during this lockdown we can reassess our words. We've heard enough. Our people have heard enough. They have been preached to, conferenced to, written to, and spoken to—but hardly ever enabled to manifest the reality of kingdom life. We even label some people as kingdom people, but when we see them close, it is about *their* kingdom, stage, ministry, and themselves.

What does the world need if not more preaching? They need a true demonstration of our preaching. They need to see the King Jesus at work with power. They need the citizens of the kingdom demonstrating who their King is. What does the following Scripture verse stir in you when you read it? *"For the creation waits with eager expectation for the children of God to be revealed"* (Romans 8:19 NIV).

The whole of creation waits for us to manifest God's power. That is why right at the beginning of this chapter I spoke about identity, and more so in previous chapters. Unless you identify with the kingdom, you will not manifest its power. More so, unless you identify as a son or daughter of God in His kingdom, you will never fully manifest all that Christ has already given you and is now available to you.

You see, in the churches we grew up in we were told we are sheep, because of the many references to God as our Shepherd in the Bible. What we didn't realize is this is a metaphor related to our *behavior*—not our identity.

Sheep have many traits that are not part of our identity. What is their greatest need? Their greatest need is pastoring. They need constant shepherding. They only need pastors, not teachers, evangelists, prophets, or apostles. Most Christians live in this dynamic of sheep led by pastors to green pastures. This mindset is so limiting. And you know where sheep live? They live outside the city gates most of the time. Is this what we are to identify with? Have you ever seen a sheep lead? No, because sheep never become leaders. They never really mature. They can never live on their own and will always need shepherding. Yes, we all need shepherding at times, but we have a higher calling. Our identity is much greater than that of a sheep.

In Romans 8:9, apostle Paul says the world is waiting to see the children of God, not the flock of God. He is talking about us, as His children, not just as mere sheep. He is inviting us to grab hold of the identity the Lord gave us to be called His children, because that's what we are (1 John 3:1).

What the world needs to see during this coronavirus pandemic and in the phasing out of it, is more sons and daughters of God who manifest who they are with power.

Only from our kingdom identity can we operate in kingdom power. The power of kingdom is for God's children. Only they inherit, sheep don't. Unless you identify as a son or daughter of the King, you will never know how to appropriate all the inheritance found in that identity.

The new identity does not succumb to the temptations of the flesh, to the ways of world or to fear. It rises above it. Apostle Paul brings it home nicely.

*Therefore, brothers and sisters, we have an obligation—but it is not to the flesh, to live according to it. For if you live according to the flesh, you will die; but if by the Spirit you put to death the misdeeds of the body, you will live. For those who are led by the Spirit of God are the children of God. The Spirit you received does not make you slaves, so that you live in fear again; rather, the Spirit you received brought about your adoption to sonship. And by him we cry, "Abba, Father." The Spirit himself testifies with our spirit that **we are**

God's children. *Now if we are children, then we are heirs—heirs of God and co-heirs with Christ, if indeed we share in his sufferings in order that we may also share in his glory* (Romans 8:12-17 NIV).

How do we know we are children of God? We allow God's Spirit to lead us. Our spirit is open to God's Spirit. We are not led by our flesh but by God's Spirit. This means we know our identity as children of God; and if children, then inheritors of all the blessings of God in Christ, so long as we follow Him.

All the promises the Bible has are for us and we can claim them because we are heirs. They belong to us as children of God. Look at apostle Peter's affirmation.

His divine power has granted to us all things that pertain to life and godliness, through the knowledge of him who called us to his own glory and excellence, by which he has granted to us his precious and very great promises, so that through them you may become partakers of the divine nature, having escaped from the corruption that is in the world because of sinful desire (2 Peter 1:3-4).

What has God's power granted us? All things—everything we need. All promises are for us and these are precious and very great. What's the purpose for these? The purpose is for us to become citizens of God's kingdom, sons and daughters of God, a new species of people who partake in the divine nature. The greatest inheritance is the divine nature, a supernatural nature. This supernatural way of life is to become our normal way of life. This is kingdom reality.

This is why Jesus wanted us to *seek the kingdom first* in terms of identity and priority. If we don't, we struggle as Christians. We do not live the fullness and abundance He came to give. And we don't manifest the true supernatural nature of God's kingdom.

How could Jesus ask us to heal the sick in every town we enter and say to the people, *"The kingdom of God has come near to you"* (Luke 10:9) if He hadn't given us the ability to do so?

The Great Commission as recorded by Mark has a very detailed manifestation aspect of the kingdom. This was to be the norm, not the exception. Jesus said:

And these signs will accompany those who believe: in my name they will cast out demons; they will speak in new tongues; they will pick up serpents with their hands; and if they drink any deadly poison, it will not hurt them; they will lay their hands on the sick, and they will recover (Mark 16:17-18).

If a pastor of a church or a ministry leader, check these for yourself. Are these signs accompanying your ministry? Are these signs proof of your church members' ministry? Take them one by one and tick them for yourself and for the people you lead. Do you and your church people:

- cast out demons,
- speak in new tongues,
- pick up deadly serpents,
- drink deadly poison, and
- lay hands on the sick?

Do you see the promised results? Do you see people delivered and healed in the name of Jesus? Is this the normal way of life for you and your church? Remember, the promise was for those who *believe*, for all of Jesus' followers.

This is how the kingdom operates. It operates with power, miracles, and with signs and wonders. The apostle Paul said it is a matter of *"righteousness and peace and joy in the Holy Spirit"* (Romans 14:17).

In the first instance Nicodemus came to Jesus at night to hear Him teach on the kingdom, barely associating with Him. Eventually he shifted from being associated to Jesus to identifying with Him. We find Nicodemus later at the tomb of Jesus as being one of His:

After these things Joseph of Arimathea, who was a disciple of Jesus, but secretly for fear of the Jews, asked Pilate that he might take away the body of Jesus, and Pilate gave him permission. So he came and took away his body. Nicodemus also, who earlier had come to Jesus by night, came bringing a mixture of myrrh and aloes, about seventy-five pounds in weight. So they took the body of Jesus and bound it in linen cloths with the spices, as is the burial custom of the Jews (John 19:38-40).

John's narrative is beautiful. He speaks of Joseph who was a disciple of Jesus, and of Nicodemus who came to Jesus by night. These two tended to the burial custom and paid for it at their highest cost.

Nicodemus brought a large quantity of myrrh and aloes, which were extremely expensive. (A quick search on the current price of myrrh gave $13,96 for 10 ml, $1,396 for one liter. Seventy-five pounds equals 33.75 liters of water, so 33.75 multiplied by $1,396 is $47,115. This is just a rough estimation revealing the massive price paid.) And Joseph gave the brand-new tomb, again a pricey real estate. Why? Both identified now with Jesus and His kingdom. And as they were identifying with the kingdom, they prioritized the kingdom as first—above all else, in practice.

If we are to have a real impact in the current climate of uncertainty in the world, we are to bring the kingdom in every realm of society. There are lots of people out there who are oppressed, sick, and fearful. We need to refocus on the kingdom and help people adjust their focus.

Let's not go back to "churchianity" as it used to be. We cannot return to a shallow and powerless mentality of the kingdom of God. It's time for the sons and daughters of God to restore kingdom priorities in their lives, and then bring restoration to others. It's time for the power of God to be manifested. It's time for signs and wonders to be the norm in the life of our church. It's time to identify and prioritize the kingdom that will stand forever (Daniel 2:44; Revelation 11:15).

ONE APPLICATION

1. What will be the one shift you will personally make in refocusing on the kingdom of God?

2. What will be the one shift your church will make in its refocusing on God's kingdom?

CHAPTER 17

REALIGN VALUES

For where your treasure is, there will your heart be also.

—Luke 12:34

The Challenges

→ *The order of the church's values is being tested during this time.*

→ *Believer's hearts are being tested in terms of value alignment.*

→ *The church loves God's purposes but are currently challenged to achieve them.*

→ *Misalignment of direction reveals misalignment in values.*

What is your definition of success? For most people success is linked to some sort of achievement in performance. If you are a pastor, success may mean your church is mature. If you are a businessperson, success may be in business growth. If you are a mother, success may come in seeing your children thrive educationally. Success can mean many things to different people.

But success is not limited to achievement. Success is also linked to fulfillment. We feel successful when we are satisfied with a met desire, when we feel fulfilled in our values. When there is fulfillment in our values and these are in alignment, we feel successful.

What are our values? If we measure success in life by the fulfillment of what we value, what do we value? If we as individuals know exactly what we value, there's a great chance to align ourselves to our values. If we as Christians and as the church understand our values, we can adhere to them and place them in order in our lives.

The current pandemic situation is a test of our values on every level, starting with our personal and family lives, our church and community life, and our wider social and business life. Why is this important? It's vital because we will do anything to be true to our values, even in the most challenging times such as these.

A value is:

- our deepest desire.
- what we are thinking of when we are not thinking of anything.
- the underlying thought of our thoughts.
- what we love deeply and allow to govern our being.
- what directs our emotional compass to do the things we do.
- connected to our heart and the desire of our heart.

Jesus defined it best when He said, *"For where your treasure is, there will your heart be also"* (Luke 12:34). The treasure He refers to here is the value I am writing about. He said most people treasure their possessions, and the temptation is real for anyone to be driven by this value. Jesus challenged His listeners to change their value system from an earthly mindset to a kingdom mindset. Only when they treasure the kingdom of God will their heart align to it. The value of the kingdom has to go from the mind, where it is often accepted as sound teaching, to the heart, where it becomes a lived-out value.

This concept is applicable to all the values we hold. Our treasure or our value is our deep desire and our heart becomes fully consumed by it.

If I value writing, for example, this is a deep desire for me that creates a positive emotional state. This means I want to experience this high emotional state on a consistent basis; and as such, this value becomes a priority for me. So I align myself to this priority and I look for different ways to engage, express, and experience that value. I make every effort to connect to my value. This value drives me to get up early in the morning at 4 a.m. without dreading it. It brings me into the fluid writing zone (anointing) for hours at a time, and I lose myself in it. My mind is consumed by ideas that run through my head and eventually find meaning in the words of my writing. My heart finds joy in my full engagement. I thrive as I immerse myself in this value.

As I mentioned, we define success differently. What we don't realize is that our definition of success affects everything we do, because it is directly linked to what we value in life. This affects our heart more than we realize and it also goes to our head. It becomes our heart's desire and our thought pattern, and our actions and our priorities become consistent with what we value.

Value Testing Begins in the Heart

The challenge of the current times is in the testing of our hearts. During the pandemic, what are our values? Do we remain consistent to our values, or do we let them go out of order? Are we aligned in our personal, family, and church life, or are we out of balance? Are we due for a realignment to our true values?

King David challenged himself and his heart to see where his values were. He asked God, *"Prove me, O LORD, and try me; test my heart and my mind"* (Psalm 26:2).

Please notice David asked God to test, to try, and to prove him. He also saw the two dimensions where his values are to be tested—first in his heart and then in his mind. He was very much in tune with himself, and this deep sense of awareness came from being just as much in tune with the Lord. Clarity in truly seeing ourselves comes when we are in tune with God.

This pattern of asking God to check his values alignment was an ongoing theme in David's relationship with God. In Psalm 139:23-24 he embraces the challenge again, *"Search me, O God, and know my heart! Try me and know my thoughts! And see if there be any grievous way in me, and lead me in the way everlasting!"*

Once again, David welcomes God's deep searching and knowing. He wants to make sure his values and motives are godly, and he embraced the testing. This is not a shallow examination. It is a deep and meaningful heart assessment and thought evaluation. He wants God to reveal to him any wrong attitudes of the heart. He wants no pretense, nor hiding. He wants full exposure of his heart. David wants his heart values to lead him to the way everlasting. His value was attached to the heavenly way. He places God and alignment to His values above all his earthly desires. He asks God to reveal any misalignment so he can be led in reordering his values properly.

Can you imagine asking God such things for yourself? Some may have done it, but most do not go really deep in their value quest. The temptation is to test our thoughts—but not our hearts. We can deal with things in our thoughts and we can even manipulate ideas. But when it comes to our hearts, eventually what we treasure there will come out. We are exposed and our values are revealed. And these may be well out of order, and an unannounced test like the current pandemic unsettles us. Why are you and your church deeply affected by the coronavirus? Is it a matter of the heart? Is it a matter of where your treasures are? Is it testing the priority order of your values?

Let me give you a contextual oversight of the current situation. Our modern life of the past 20-30 years has been pretty good especially in the developed countries. Never in history have we had it better than during this period. When you look at history, you see many accounts of war, natural disasters, famine, and poverty. Generation after generation had it rough. Life expectancy was low and life was tough. Most people were working hard and yet they were poor; while the few wealthy people enjoyed life. There was discrimination at every level and a sense of hopelessness throughout history.

Fast-forward to our generation and things are totally different. In most regions of the world, there's equality in almost every aspect of life and opportunities for everyone to excel and enjoy life. Never in history have we had more possessions than now. Never before have we been so affluent.

Think about housing, for example, and how good it is with all the modern services at our fingertips. Look at our travel options—car ownership, public transport, and worldwide flights. What about healthcare? We have available to us medical centers, hospitals, and medicine. Security? Our countries, cities, and our homes are safe. Food is readily available and affordable, both raw and cooked, fresh and frozen. Business opportunities are only limited by our perception, numerous possibilities are available. Take everything else—jobs, education, clothing, personal care, Internet, entertainment, sports, spirituality, and I can go on and on—all accessible to almost everyone worldwide.

Our awareness has to be that life has been good. The awareness has to go one step deeper and make us realize that our hearts have been attached to something other than His kingdom. We now value conveniences and we have developed an entitlement attitude toward them. We love luxury, comfort, security, and adventure.

Why do we change cars so often even though the current one has plenty to offer? Why do we constantly change our wardrobe, our looks, and even our homes? The "consumer mentality" of this current world we live in has sneaked into our hearts, and its values have become our values, its desires our desires, and its ways, our ways.

The coronavirus surprised us in an unpleasant way and we overreact as if we are small children. Our toys are taken away. Our comfort is unsettled, our security is threatened, and our finances are taking a hit. It is disruptive and we don't like it.

Why is the coronavirus affecting us? Why is it agitating believers? Why is it unsettling our churches? Why is this such a challenge?

Let me tell you why. It is because our hearts are connected to our possessions. We value our possessions in our heart, which drives our everyday attitudes and actions. We get so wrapped up in things, that we don't even realize they have become the driving force of what we do and how we live.

I quoted Jesus' connection between the treasures (values) and our hearts as recorded in Luke 12:34. Before He said that our hearts are where our values are, He told us why. He said everything is connected to our possessions, which are corrupting our hearts. In Luke 12:33 (NIV) Jesus says, *"Sell your possessions and give to the poor. Provide purses for yourselves that will not wear out, a treasure in heaven that will never fail, where no thief comes near and no moth destroys."*

It's a similar challenge as the one Jesus gave the rich young ruler (Luke 18:22). Disconnect from your possessions, in your heart. They are not true values. They are misleading you. They are deceiving you. They are misaligning your life.

All our earthly possessions can and will wear out, they can be easily stolen and destroyed. Look at your losses over the years. Could you do anything to prevent them?

Do you know what still stands the test of time? What you did for the Lord, the investment you made in heaven—the inexhaustible, dependable, undiminishing, unfailing, never decreasing, and safe treasure. It is the best investment because it never loses its value. It is eternal. We have an opportunity to use the temporary for the eternal.

I am not saying we shouldn't prosper. I am not saying we shouldn't want wealth. They are our promises from God and we are to grab hold of them. But the reason has to be greater than our personal and family pleasures. The purpose of wealth is distribution. The purpose of being prosperous is to advance the kingdom of God. It is stewarding the affairs of God on earth. It is partnering with God to bring heavenly solutions to earthly problems. It is in bringing the kingdom into every heart. And the coronavirus invites us to reassess and realign.

We needed this recalibration. The church needed this changeover. Consumerism has crept into our lives and into our churches. We value what the world values. We pattern our lives and our churches after the world. We value the modern building, the comfortable furniture, the stage lighting, the culture, the loving music, the friendly preaching, the Sunday show—and we measure our church experience in earthly terms.

That's why the apostle Paul has challenged us in not conforming to the world. He wrote, *"Do not be conformed to this world, but be transformed by the renewal of your mind, that by testing you may discern what is the will of God, what is good and acceptable and perfect"* (Romans 12:2).

Do not adhere to the patterns and values of the world. Renew your mind to the heavenly values. Learn the will of God, test your life and live by His will. Discern. As Christians we have the ability to discern what value is godly and what is not. We can discern the will of God. And His will is good, acceptable, and perfect.

Why is it that we choose otherwise? Why do we accept the not so good, the not so acceptable, and the not so perfect? It is because our values are misaligned. Our values are not heavenly, but worldly. We have been conformed and molded into the patterns of the world. And when the world is turned upside down with a pandemic, we act just like it does. It disrupts us and we don't like it.

We ought to know better. We ought to live better. We ought to have higher values. We ought to prove our values in this time. We were happy to teach people biblical concepts, but we expected them to live by their personal convictions. We haven't drilled biblical values regarding possessions deep enough into their hearts. We only worked at the intellect level, and they only accepted them as good teachings.

King David said, *"I have stored up your word in my heart, that I might not sin against you"* (Psalm 119:11) In his heart is where David deposited, hid, and treasured the word of God. It was a value he was going to live by. He opened his heart and took it in deep. David saved it there, treasured it, and aligned his life according to it. He treasured it above everything else so he could remain pure, holy, and not sin against God.

Attachment to possessions is sinful. It is idolatry. Unless we see it that way, we will not lose our attraction to it. In his discipleship teaching to Timothy, the apostle Paul made him aware of this trap. He wrote, *"For the love of money is the root of all kinds of evil. And some people, craving money, have wandered from the true faith and pierced themselves with many sorrows"* (1 Timothy 6:10 New Living Translation).

Why would anyone desire to tap into the source of all kinds of evil? Why would a Christian treasure that? The danger is twofold: it seduces people away from their faith and causes people a lot of piercing pain.

Our values expose our loves. At the center of the Christian message is the love for God and the love for others. If our love for God is not in order, all other loves are messed up and misaligned.

We are tested to see if our love for our possessions has climbed up the ladder and pushed our true love of God from its primary place.

Allow this period of testing to go deep in your assessment of your values alignment. Ask the Lord, just like King David to lead you in a way that is everlasting (Psalm 139:24).

Value Alignment Begins in the Heart

I grew up with a father who loved the Lord in his heart and his love for God was always on his lips. I will never forget one of his favorite Scripture passages he memorized and often recited to us. This beautiful poetry has the secrets of aligning our hearts with God's treasures:

Agree with God, and be at peace; thereby good will come to you.
Receive instruction from his mouth,
and lay up his words in your heart.
If you return to the Almighty you will be built up;
if you remove injustice far from your tents,
if you lay gold in the dust,
and gold of Ophir among the stones of the torrent-bed,
then the Almighty will be your gold and your precious silver.
For then you will delight yourself in the Almighty
and lift up your face to God.
You will make your prayer to him,
and he will hear you, and you will pay your vows.
You will decide on a matter, and it will be established for you,
and light will shine on your ways.
For when they are humbled you say, "It is because of pride";
but he saves the lowly.
He delivers even the one who is not innocent,
who will be delivered through the cleanness of your hands.

—Job 22:21-30

Let's pause and reflect on the wisdom of this tested man, Job, and his heart alignment with God. His instructions are well tested through his difficult journey of losing everything, but keeping his alignment of values. Job admonishes us to:

1. Agree with God.
2. Be at peace.
3. Receive instructions from God's mouth.
4. Lay up God's words in your heart.
5. Return to the Almighty to be built up.
6. Remove injustice from your circle of influence.
7. Throw your gold to the ground.
8. Lay down your gold—give up love of money.
9. Throw your precious gold and stones into the river.
10. Make God your gold and your precious silver.
11. Delight yourself in God and lift up your face to Him.
12. When you pray, He will hear.
13. Keep your promises to Him.
14. You will succeed in everything you do.
15. God's light will shine ahead of you.
16. When you ask God to help those in trouble, He will save them.
17. Every sinner will be rescued, because your hands are pure.

Job's values are aligned to God in his heart because he agreed with God through obedience by laying up God's words in his heart. He returned to God to receive instruction and recalibration. Some of what he had to do was remove injustice and let go of all the valuable possessions he had. The key for Job was to make God his most precious possession, greater than any precious gold or silver. It was to make God his full delight. Only then can success come in his life in every area including prayer, keeping promises, having light in decisions, helping those in trouble, rescuing sinners, and in fact succeeding in all he does.

Values Alignment Brings Life Alignment

Life alignment starts with values alignment. If we are to be living life to the potential the Lord has for us, we must become sons and daughters of the kingdom of God whose primary value is His kingdom.

Our human behavior is linked directly to our meaning in life. The most important factor in deciding our meaning in life is our identity—what and with whom we identify. This is the driving force behind everything we value and everything we do. The following five stages reveal insights into our human behavior beginning with our own identity.

Five Stages to Reveal Our Identity

1. Realign from achieved identity to received identity.

See what kind of love the Father has given to us, that we should be called children of God; and so we are. The reason why the world does not know us is that it did not know him (1 John 3:1).

The world suffers today without aligned values because it lacks true identity. The people around us do not know who they are in the eyes of God. They do not have a real sense of godly identity.

The current disruption with the pandemic unsettles them severely because there is no true anchor to their life. There is no transcendent identity.

Every day people are working hard to try to *achieve* their identity. They are consumed by becoming the manager, the patron, the rich, the influencer, the best, the expert, the fastest, etc. They get into the program that says, do this and then you get your identity. Earn this degree and then you get this job. Finish this and then you get this title. Climb this ladder and you will be the one at the top. Go through these seven steps and you will find yourself. Their identity is linked to their achieved performance because this is the norm of the world.

How we view ourselves and how we position ourselves in this world is critical to understand if we want to be all we are meant to be. This is powerful because our conscious or unconscious behavior will make every effort to remain consistent to how we view ourselves.

The power of our identity infiltrates every part of our experiences in life. When it comes to Christian identity, the concept is simple. Our identity is as sons and daughters of God—that's who we are. The world cannot see this identity because they don't recognize God as their Father.

God is the identity giver. He gave identity to Adam, and then asked him to give identity to the animals, and then to his wife. Adam could only do that if his identity was sorted out first. Only out of a place of a healthy and true identity could Adam give identity to others.

When we are born into this world we get our identities from our fathers. When we are born again, we are born of above, which means we get a new identity from our God, our heavenly Father. Identity is given, not achieved. You can never achieve such an identity.

The problem we have in churches before we even look at the world is that our people *know* their identity *at the mind level*, but don't fully *know it in their heart to live by it.* That is why so many of them are afraid during this pandemic.

How many believers have a victim mentality? Do we realize how this messes up every value in their lives? It starts with messing up their perspective, then their thoughts, then the meaning they give those thoughts, and then the emotions that follow. Why is that? They haven't fully appropriated the identity God gave them.

2. Realign from common perspective to higher perspective.

Do not be conformed to this world, but be transformed by the renewal of your mind, that by testing you may discern what is the will of God, what is good and acceptable and perfect (Romans 12:2).

We come back to this verse once again in this chapter. This verse is insightful to understand our perspective. Perspective is the way we look at everything, the lenses we put on, the worldview we have—perspective is how we see things.

The invitation here is to be renewed in our mind to a godly viewpoint. It is to rise up to God's perspective on everything. It is to realign from a common earthly perspective to a higher, godly perspective. It means to see things as God sees them. As a son or daughter, you can have this. If your identity is clear, then you embrace the perspective that comes from that identity.

3. Realign from our thoughts to His thoughts.

"For who has understood the mind of the Lord so as to instruct him?" But we have the mind of Christ (1 Corinthians 2:16).

The perspective we have on everything determines our thoughts, influencing their quality or lack of it.

Because the victim identity is real, if we see ourselves as a victim of circumstance or life, it will have a direct impact on our perspective. Our perspective will be that life is unfair because our identity is immersed in victimhood. Our perspective influences our thought patterns and is fueled by it. In our thoughts we gather evidence on why our perspective is accurate.

If I believe I am a victim, I will do all that I can to assemble evidence in my thoughts why that is true. My thoughts become an extension of my perspective. They are the themes I focus on and they become a reflection of the evidence gathered to support my victim perspective.

As such, if my identity is healthily rooted in Christ, I have a totally different perspective from people who see themselves as victims. I have the perspective that I have inherited the mind of Christ. This means that my thinking is no longer my thinking, but His. It means I can have the thought patterns that govern the mind of Christ, not mine. It means I make a conscious choice to change my ideas to align with His truth rather than bending the truth to align with my ideas.

When I have a healthy identity in Christ my perspective will be riddled with appreciation, gratitude, and joy. Naturally my thoughts will gather evidence as to why I should be grateful, appreciative, and joyful. And then my thoughts will give healthy, godly meaning to all that I experience. My emotional state is therefore quite balanced and good. This makes me, generally speaking, a godly aligned person.

4. Realign meaning from old to new.

Therefore, if anyone is in Christ, he is a new creation. The old has passed away; behold, the new has come (2 Corinthians 5:17).

When our identity in Christ is real, we become a new creation. Nothing of the old should be there, all must be new. Our way of interpreting our thoughts is no longer a worldly way, an old nature way; rather, it is new. We give way to the new by dismissing the old. Our old nature has been crucified with Christ and the new has come, behold all is new. The meaning we give to everything is now aligned to the new identity.

Why is this important? It is important because the meaning we give our thoughts directly affects our emotions. Every thought has a meaning attached to it—the way we interpret that thought and meaning creates the emotions we feel.

How can people become emotionally aligned, especially during this time when thoughts can run wild with fear attached to the pandemic? They become aware of their thought patterns. They watch their thoughts. They understand the flow.

There is a cascading effect from thoughts, to meaning, and to emotions. Emotions come from the meaning we give our thoughts, from the stories and interpretations we frame in our minds. And the thoughts come from our perspective about who we are—our identity. It all aligns nicely.

New creations—us—have a balanced state of emotions because the meaning associates with thoughts that are linked to the perspective that comes from our identity (2 Corinthians 5:17).

5. Realign emotions from guide to gauge.

Therefore, preparing your minds for action, and being sober-minded, set your hope fully on the grace that will be brought to you at the revelation of Jesus Christ (1 Peter 1:13).

I remember reading somewhere a powerful saying, "Pleasure is the measure of your treasure." The emotion of pleasure is a gauge that tells you what you love.

Christians should not be driven by emotions, although many are. In this frantic period of history the challenge is in regulating the overwhelming emotions created by fear from the coronavirus uncertainty. We should not allow our emotions to overpower our God-given identity, assurance, and our intelligence. We should not allow others to control the direction of our lives—not the media, not the politicians, and not the views of people around us.

Apostle Peter calls us to prepare our minds, to have our minds ready for action in any circumstance. What he means is to be alert and full of self-control, to gird up the loins of your mind. In simple terms he is saying to think straight, keep a clear head, be serious, and not to be affected by emotions.

Our underlying emotion should be hope. This hope should be set completely on the blessings of God revealed in Christ Jesus. This hope comes from the meaning we give our thoughts that are influenced by our perspective of our identity.

Every emotion we experience should be a gauge for us, not a guide. Emotions should report to us, not we to them. Our emotions come from the meaning we give our thoughts and they highlight our perspective and ultimately our identity. They should help us check if our identity is truly linked to our values.

Once we understand how our values are linked to our identity we can align this understanding to any value we hold dear.

So if one of our core values is the family unit, it means we identify with that value as a husband, wife, child, grandparent, or a mixture of these. That healthy aspect of our God-given identity offers us the quality of our perspective. The quality of our perspective toward the family influences what we think about, what we focus on, and is directly associated with the meaning we give those thoughts, and hence our emotional state.

When I value the family unit, my perspective toward my role as a father comes from the identity God gave me as the head of my household, the priest and the king unto God. I filter everything through my identity that gives me a healthy perspective. My thoughts are aligned with that perspective; and the meaning I give my thoughts will bring healthy emotions because everything is well aligned.

In a misaligned world we are to bring spiritual alignment. To bring spiritual alignment to others, we ourselves have to have it first. The world around us needs alignment more than ever. We, the church, are best placed to bring this to them.

Learn this lesson now during this pandemic, and realign your values so you can help others rise up and take hold of their true identity. The steps highlighted in this chapter will work on all Christian values you have including grace, hope, faith, love, justice, joy, and peace. They all spring from our identity in Christ and ripple down to our perspective, thoughts, meaning, and emotions. And these will bring a true sense of fulfillment in a godly values-driven life.

ONE APPLICATION

1. What is the one thing you will personally apply in realigning the values in your life?

2. What is the one thing your church will apply in realigning its values?

CHAPTER 18

REWRITE THE NARRATIVE

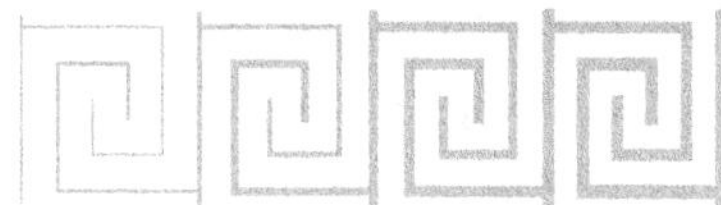

But I am afraid that as the serpent deceived Eve by his cunning, your thoughts will be led astray from a sincere and pure devotion to Christ.

—2 Corinthians 11:3

The Challenges

→ *The church is currently plagued by skewed narratives.*

→ *The church can be easily influenced by conspiracies.*

→ *The media hype is against the church.*

→ *The church must be the light in this dark period.*

Who speaks to you the most? Your spouse, children, parents, business partner, boss? No. *You* speak to you the most. What do you tell yourself? Stories. What type of stories? Stories you make up in your mind by the meaning you give to your thoughts.

If we speak to ourselves the most, we must become aware of our self-narrative. What do we say to ourselves? What is the narrative of our lives, and what is the narrative of our every day?

In a world full of narratives easily communicated through the digital media, how do we keep our narrative sound? How influenced are we by what we hear and also by what we communicate?

This current period of history has some really dark narratives. As Christians and as the church we are not spared from these. We are even tempted to engage in some of these and make them our convincing truths.

Some of the stories out there tell us this is the end of the world. Others will say the antichrist is about to be revealed and "One World Order" is around the corner. Others read into COVID-19 as the opportunity to have everyone chipped through a nano vaccine and traced by the timely launching of 5G—this being the sign of the beast. And there's a lot more skewed theories out there watched and endorsed by millions of people, including a high percentage of Christians. It's like the Christians are actually looking for these stories.

I have seen churches in this time change their narratives and messages to fit the conspiracies trend. I have heard pastors preaching doom and gloom messages and not holding back from their misaligned rhetoric. I even heard them changing their stories, going back on some things they said just weeks before, not being concerned about the roller coaster of emotions and fears they bring to those listening. It is messy out there and the church is not spared.

The Story You Live By

The story you live by is the story you tell yourself. This narrative is extremely powerful because it is very, very real and it triggers you into different emotional states. There is a saying, "If you are a hammer, everything looks like a nail." That's the hammer's truth.

It only sees nails regardless of whether they are or not. Our narrative can be just like that. It can put a view of the world that is unique to us on just about anything. And then we also have the challenge to healthily respect all of the narratives around us.

Bring COVID-19 into this discussion and the whole scenario changes. People will have narratives affected by shutdowns, mask-wearing, restrictions, fear of the second wave of the pandemic, and new rules that come into play. These trigger changing narratives in people's thoughts and also in their experiences.

When we become aware that the story we tell ourselves us affects not only us but those we share our life and experiences with, we also develop a sense of awareness toward the stories of others. As we engage with people around us, we enter their world of their narrative. The mission is to have a healthy respect of their narrative and even explore where it is coming from.

The story we tell ourselves either amplifies or minimizes what we see in the world. If your story is immersed in family, you will notice all the wonderful aspects out in the world. You will notice mothers, fathers, children, grandparents and their activities. If your story is connected to sports, everything you see has a sports connotation. If you are pregnant, you notice all the pregnant women and all the parents with children.

Our narrative is the most powerful contributor to what we notice or stop noticing in our environment. As we drive around, walk, shop, or any other activity, we notice aspects connected deeply to our story. Our story expands in every environment to notice things that align to it.

Why is this important? This is important because we need to become sensitive in our awareness of our narrative. Otherwise we get trapped in the echoes of our historical data. We can easily live in the shadows of our experiences that shape and define us.

What I am about to share here with you is vital to you framing healthy narratives in life. If you can get this, and I pray you will, you will have amazing clarity in the narratives you choose to live by.

None of us experience reality directly. What we experience is our experience of reality. We live out our way of experiencing that reality. Different people experience the same reality differently. That is why everyone has a different story of that same reality. And that story is very real for each person, because it is attached to the experience they have in that story.

Our story is made up of our values, our beliefs, and our assumptions. These assumptions are the convenient interpretations we gave our experiences. These have then become beliefs and values we live by. All aspects of our memories, including joyful moments or painful experiences, can be quite distorted.

If you only think about what you remember from when you were a kid, you will see they are not true facts of reality. They are your experiences and your assumptions of that reality. Your brother or sister experienced that reality differently—and your parents, radically different.

We distort memories according to our experiences in life right now or in trying to move forward. That is why a sound awareness of the story we tell ourselves is important.

If we understand that we only experience our own experience of reality, it means we have the power to reset our narrative. We can redefine and redesign our story going forward. In the future decisions we make in life about our lives, our families, our churches, and our business, we need to watch the narrative we tell ourselves. The quality of our narrative affects the quality of our choices.

This is a call to arms to rewrite your narrative. Many people live their story by default, not questioning what goes on in the stories they tell themselves. They get trapped in the past stories that cloud their current reality.

What do you tell yourself? Is your narrative bringing you joy, assurance, fulfillment, and love? Or is it bringing fear, disruption, frustration, and hell? The story you tell yourself determines what you experience in life. The story you help others write for themselves will help them lift up what they also experience in life.

How immersed is your narrative in spirituality? Do you have a conscious connection with the divine in your everyday thought pattern? Is the Lord's presence and His reality governing your thinking? Are you looking for His truth in your story? Where does He fit in your present story and especially in your future story?

You see, the Lord does not reside in your ego story. He does not take part in our selfish nature narrative. It's not who we truly are in Him. He is not part of the ego story we author about ourselves and daily entertain ourselves with. God demands a reconfiguration of our narrative. He demands us to press the reset button and restart the next phase of our lives immersed in His truth, because that is the real narrative worth writing.

The Real Narrative Is the Truth

If our story is so subjective to our conditioning and our perception of reality, and so is the story of all around us, then what is the real story? Our story can only be accurate, truthful, and real when we have the absolute truth in us. Our narrative is genuine in its full capacity only when it springs out of unconditional truth.

When Jesus prayed for His disciples, He asked God the Father to bring, dedicate or sanctify, them by the truth, which was His word. Jesus said, *"Sanctify them in the truth; your word is truth"* (John 17:17).

All other truth is relative. All other truth is subjective. Only when a person is made holy in God's word can he or she begin to live in the truth. When that truth is a way of life for followers of Jesus, their story is filtered through that truth and gradually becomes truthful. All other narrative is selfish, subjective, and distorted.

Why do people avoid this narrative? They bypass it because it is confronting. It demands soberness of the mind. It demands spiritual awakening and spiritual watch. It demands accepting the holiness of God and letting go of carnal thoughts. It demands authenticity to the core of our being, and that is very uncomfortable. But that is the only story worth living. We know that, but so few run with it.

In this challenging time, people need the truth. Members of the body of Christ need to be made holy through God's truth. Their narrative has to be immersed in truth, because Jesus is our Truth. Among all the noise of all the stories out there, Christianity's story is the best; not because you and I say it, but because it is the truth. It shines brighter than any darkness. We need to live in the truth and live out the narrative of this truth to others.

The Beginning of Our Story

Every story has a beginning. Because God created everything, there is a God-beginning to everything. And if we want our narrative to align with God's truth, we must search for that story as the base for our current description.

To assist us in framing our truth story, Jesus invites us to go back to the beginning. He used this method several times referring back to God's Law, which He came to fulfill (Matthew 5:17).

Let me refresh for you the story about divorce and how Jesus brought them back to the beginning.

And Pharisees came up and in order to test him asked, "Is it lawful for a man to divorce his wife?" He answered them, "What did Moses command you?" They said, "Moses allowed a man to write a certificate of divorce and to send her away." And Jesus said to them, "Because of your hardness of heart he wrote you this commandment. But from the beginning of creation, 'God made them male and female.' 'Therefore a man shall leave his father and mother and hold fast to his wife, and the two shall become one flesh.' So they are no longer two but one flesh. What therefore God has joined together, let not man separate" (Mark 10:2-9).

An inquiry is brought to Jesus by the Pharisees, about the divorce story, how this can be written in an acceptable way. He sends them back to Moses' written narrative. They find some convenient truth in that narrative and seem to be running with it. Jesus purposely took them to this narrative to show them where the problem lies.

He says in essence, yes, that story is important but that's not the original story. The story you refer to was rewritten for you because you had heart issues. It was reframed, and it shifted from the original truth. But you liked it and took it on without going back to the beginning where the true teaching is found. You started the divorce story and made it a favorable way of life for you, not from the beginning. You left the most essential part out. You preferred to have the door open out of marriage, through divorce, by Moses' concession of giving the wife a divorce certificate. That was the story you entertained and promoted. And that became your story.

Jesus said that in the beginning, God's story for humanity was different and the Pharisees overlooked that. God made male and female to be married, to leave their parents, and to be one for life. In fact the marriage story gives no license to anyone to break a marriage. What God has united, no one is to separate. That is the truth of the matter.

If Christianity was to embrace this truth of the marriage story, then this would be the way of life. The narratives of people's marriages and their views on marriages would be truthful and abundantly blessed. But when the story is rewritten to suit various situations, then those stories are taken away from the truth and mess up many multiple lives.

That is why Jesus always brings us back to the beginning of the story, to His truth on the matter, because this is the only one that should really inspire and guide our life story. Everything else is not the full truth. And that is why there is so much suffering and anguish in the stories of Christians. The narratives we tell ourselves and we choose to live by are not based on God's original truth.

The End of Our Story

When we incorporated our ministry here in Australia, one of my wise counselors advised me to have the end in mind from day one. He instructed me to have a constitution that spells out clearly the end and to structure it from the end's perspective.

His advice was invaluable. It brought a healthy perspective. It forced us to go through various scenarios and consider what is ultimately valued in this ministry. It was an exercise that defined our engagement in the ministry. Knowing that you have a say in how the story ends gives you confidence to write the plot chapter by chapter.

When it comes to our life story, we know the end. We know how our book ends. We've read the final chapter. We know the ending right now.

We win!

Jesus wins in the end, and we are hidden in His victory. In fact, He's already won—we just need to live out that victory.

Apostle Paul knew this. He wrote, *"But thanks be to God, who gives us the victory through our Lord Jesus Christ"* (1 Corinthians 15:57).

The victory is ours and the story ends well. If we know that, we ought to live from that position. We need to reverse engineer our story. Live in the present tense from our future state. That is a true reality most Christians don't take on.

Remember, we are seated with Christ right now in heavenly places (Ephesians 2:6). This is not just a future part of our story, it is the reality of our story right now. But we have to look at it from the end perspective, otherwise it makes no sense right now.

Our end is glorious and real, and we can engage in our end story every day. Our minds should have the end perspective turned on at all times. Our end victory lenses should be the ones we look through at our current events.

If we write the story in reverse, the coronavirus does not unbalance us nor torment us. We know it is just a hiccup on the way. Our story is eternal. We have a duty to help our people rewrite their narrative from an eternal, winning perspective. That means leading them in truth.

The Wrong Narrative Leads to Deception

What is the opposite of the truth? A lie. Who is the father of lies? The devil. To bear a child you need a mother and a father. If the devil is the father of lies, who is the mother of lies that births the lie? We are. We become intimate with the devil to birth the lie. Awful, isn't it? Disgraceful. That's how lies are born, out of that oneness with the devil.

How do we get our narrative so wrong, so untrue? By allowing doubts to creep into our thought pattern. This is the pattern apostle

Paul warned us against when he reminded us about how the devil deceived Eve.

> *But I am afraid that **as the serpent deceived Eve** by his cunning, **your thoughts will be led astray** from a sincere and pure devotion to Christ* (2 Corinthians 11:3).

The devil deceived Eve by his cunning ways that were working in her mind to doubt the words of God. Let's recall Genesis 3:1:

> *Now the serpent was more crafty than any other beast of the field that the LORD God had made. He said to the woman, "Did God actually say, 'You shall not eat of any tree in the garden'?"*

The devil is playing with Eve's narrative. He didn't present an obvious deception. He wasn't lying to her face. She would have picked it up straight away. He craftily engaged in a "thought-provoking" discussion.

He gently challenged her story with doubt. Is your story really the truth? Will you truly live by that? Did God really tell you that, or is that how you are interpreting it? Think again.

Look at how craftily the devil rewrites God's words, the true narrative, "Can you not eat from any fruit of the garden?" He framed the question in a way Eve had to answer in affirmative. This affirmative opened the door for her to doubt. He knew she would reveal that they could eat of all the fruit, except the fruit of the tree in the middle. There was only one they couldn't eat from, but the devil generalized it. He distorted the story and Eve allowed the new narrative to enter. And just like that, she was deceived.

Paul reminds us the danger is still real and the serpent still wants to deceive us in our thoughts and lead us astray from a pure devotion to Christ, from a pure narrative of who Christ is.

The world we live in right now is full of deception. Christianity is not spared. Believers are taken down with distorted narratives every day, and more so during this pandemic when the media has run wild. Why? It's because they allow doubt to come into their minds. It's the devil's cunning and crafty way to get to our story and mess it up. Once he gets us to doubt, he will deceive us.

The devil is lying to us and wants our story to be scattered with lies, to make our journey difficult, so we give up. I developed a saying:

> The lie you listen to becomes the lie you tolerate.
> The lie you tolerate becomes the lie you accept.
> The lie you accept becomes the lie you memorize.
> The lie you memorize becomes the lie you promote.
> And the lie you promote becomes the truth you live by.

Do you see how deception works? From listening or imagining a doubtful story, then we tolerate it, accept it, learn it, promote it, and in the end we are deceived as it becomes our truth. The lie was turned into truth for us. What is that? It is deception, self-deception. It is being led astray from a sincere and pure devotion to Christ.

Our role as spiritual leaders in this world full of false narratives is to bring spiritual truth. Speaking as a pastor, we need to nip it in the bud for people and not allow them to entertain silly stories that will eventually deceive them. We need to be on guard and blow the trumpets. Wrong narratives bring deceptions.

Let Your Story Shine

The world is watching the church. Your city and your neighborhood are watching your church. People who know you, watch you. They want to see how you and your faith and your church handle the current situation. They expect clear direction and sound leadership.

If the church doesn't have this, then who will? Jesus was clear in commissioning us; He said:

"You are the light of the world. A city set on a hill cannot be hidden. Nor do people light a lamp and put it under a basket, but on a stand, and it gives light to all in the house. In the same way, let your light shine before others, so that they may see your good works and give glory to your Father who is in heaven" (Matthew 5:14-16).

God's children have a mandate to be the light of the world. We have a mandate to be the city on a hill, not hiding away but in full visibility. We *cannot* be hidden. We are to give light to this dark period of history. Jesus was so clear in what is expected of us as the light of the world. We are to shine before others in such a way that they see our actions and our works; and by seeing these good works, they get a glimpse of the glory of God. This will bring them to giving glory to God!

What is your story like? Is it a doom and gloom story just like the rest of the world's? Is it consumed by fear, panic, and a fatalist outlook? Is your story more like an old nature story? Is your story more connected to the physical and the here and now?

Or is your story rewritten by the words of Jesus?

Does your story shine Jesus? Is your narrative immersed in light? Are you guiding people into the light? Do you give light to and through your church, to everyone in your circle of influence? Does your story ultimately bring glory to God?

You know you have the truth. You know God's story is true. When His story is our story, there is nothing to prove. The truth does not need defending. It sits so much higher than anything else, and it needs no props. The truth is in itself standing because the truth is not a term or an ideal, the truth is a person—Jesus Christ.

Our call is to tell the story of Jesus as the absolute truth. Our call is to live out this story.

Is it uncomfortable? Yes, to some. It shouldn't be, but it is. If a pastor, I encourage you to get ready to preach the word in full truth. Prepare not to be liked. Prepare to be rejected. It will be confronting and unpleasant for those hearing it. This is what apostle Paul wanted his spiritual son to do:

Preach the word of God. Be prepared, whether the time is favorable or not. Patiently correct, rebuke, and encourage your people with good teaching (2 Timothy 4:2 New Living Translation).

This is what apostle Paul said just before he spoke about consumer type storytellers. He told Timothy to preach the word of God. That was the narrative to be on Timothy's lips. And this instruction is timeless. Whether the time is favorable or not, whether we're in great times or troubled times, whether you feel fantastic or you feel down, whether you are received or not, whether you like it or not, you need to be prepared to always preach the truth.

Apostle Paul's instructions are quite challenging: to preach, patiently correct, and rebuke, and also encourage your listeners with good teaching. Two of the three instructions have to do with realignment, reorder, and recalibration—correct and rebuke. Only one is highly positive—encourage. And then Paul gives Timothy insight into what stories will attract people:

For the time is coming when people will not endure sound teaching, but having itching ears they will accumulate for themselves teachers to suit their own passions (2 Timothy 4:3).

The time has come when people cannot endure sound teachings. It is here upon us. People cannot bear the truth of the gospel anymore—church people that is, not people of the world. They would rather not hear it. It doesn't stimulate their passions. They will go elsewhere chasing narrative congruent to their worldly desires. They will chase fairy tales that entertain their passions.

The Story Within

I end this chapter with a powerful insight into the story we keep within us. In this outer world chaos, we need stability within. Our inner story has to remain sound and undeterred. Otherwise, our inner world cannot keep up with what's going on outside.

As we feel restricted, limited, locked down, and forced to wear masks, our freedoms are threatened. When these freedoms are threatened, we behave in ways we are not used to, our psychology changes. It plays with our heads.

When we listen to the stories around us, we begin to hear extremes in people's narratives. It is only natural that these can unsettle our inner thoughts. We then tend to behave like children who are afraid. What do we do in these circumstances?

A young child in circumstances such as these would look for his or her parent. They need assurance, care, and want to feel safe. They want to hear that everything will be okay. But that source is outside them.

We believers can go within to what God has deposited in us and is currently developing in us. We can tap into what He is growing us into becoming. Who are we becoming through this era? What will we carry from within, outside? The narrative in our hearts can be immersed in our identity in Christ. Our assurance, safety, and future outlook can be secured in Christ. We can bring divine internal order in this world full of chaos.

When we do that, our inner state is at peace. The Lord of peace is, as promised, our Peace (Micah 5:5). The story we narrate within is His story, His promises, and His eternal perspective. We cannot ignore people who are fascinated by noisy, ungodly narratives out there. We must share no other but God's story with everyone.

ONE APPLICATION

1. What will you take on as the one thing in rewriting your personal narrative?

2. What will you take on as the one thing for your church in rewriting its narrative?

CHAPTER 19

RISE TO THE OCCASION

*For it is time for judgment to begin at the household of God;
and if it begins with us, what will be the outcome
for those who do not obey the gospel of God?*

—1 Peter 4:17

The Challenges

→ *The world is watching Christianity for perspective.*

→ *Church people are waiting for godly leadership.*

→ *The church must undergo the process to attain its purpose.*

→ *The church has an opportunity to come into its finest hour.*

At the beginning of this book the challenge of the coronavirus pandemic was overwhelmingly high. The very first chapter was an invitation for the church to embrace and engage in the challenge.

As we unpacked the many Bible-immersed applicable lessons, we were taken on a journey of awareness, learning, conviction, and shifting. And as this journey approaches the end, we begin to realize more and more that the current situation presents us Christians and the Church as a whole limitless opportunities.

In this final chapter I invite you to come up higher and to rise to the occasion—as an individual, as a family, and as a church family.

The study has presented countless insights with deep spiritual truths carefully placed in there by the Holy Spirit to bring you to a higher understanding of Christ and your identity in Him.

You have the opportunity now to apply these in your personal Christian walk and also in those you may lead in church, at home, and your workplace.

You may be tempted to take it just as good teachings and leave it there. Please don't do that. Do not return to the pre-COVID-19 mindset. You cannot. Your church cannot.

God has been doing something in this time and in this space. You were part of it because God was developing something in you and in your church. He is allowing us to go through a process to attain His purposes.

Rise to the *Process* to Get to the *Purpose*

Recently I met with a seasoned leader of our city. He leads an organization that restores young people from addiction. When I asked him what the Lord was telling Him during this time, he told me it had to do with accepting the process God takes us through en route to attaining His purposes. That is the whole heart of God, and that became the heart of this mature leader's ministry.

He was right. He mentioned briefly to me the story of Naaman and Elisha. To attain the purposes God had for them, they had to go through a process.

Naaman's story is intriguing. He was the commander of the army of the king of Syria and had contracted leprosy. His life was at stake. He finds out about Elisha, God's prophet, from his wife's slave. Elisha could cure him so Naaman makes the journey to Elisha's house. While he is outside, Elisha's messenger comes out and tells Naaman to go and wash himself seven times in the Jordan River and he would be healed (2 Kings 5:1-10).

God is inviting Naaman, through Elisha and his messenger, into a process that would bring healing—the purpose he came for. Naaman wanted the result (purpose), but not the process. Look at his reaction. Look also at the result of entering the process:

But Naaman was angry and went away, saying, "Behold, I thought that he would surely come out to me and stand and call upon the name of the Lord his God, and wave his hand over the place and cure the leper. Are not Abana and Pharpar, the rivers of Damascus, better than all the waters of Israel? Could I not wash in them and be clean?" So he turned and went away in a rage. But his servants came near and said to him, "My father, it is a great word the prophet has spoken to you; will you not do it? Has he actually said to you, 'Wash, and be clean'?" So he went down and dipped himself seven times in the Jordan, according to the word of the man of God, and his flesh was restored like the flesh of a little child, and he was clean (2 Kings 5:11-14).

The first reaction was like ours with the coronavirus. Why isn't God just sorting this? Why doesn't He just say a word and it's done with? Why do we have to go through this pandemic?

There is a process that brings the purposes of God into being. Naaman had to accept God's process, be obedient to it, and live it out. When he accepted the process and engaged in it, he got to the purpose—he was clean and healed.

Jesus applied the same method with His disciples. He said, *"Follow me, and I will make you fishers of men"* (Matthew 4:19). He invites them into a process—follow Me, for a purpose—to become fishers of men. In the process of following Him, He would *make* them. Without the process the purpose cannot be reached.

The taking of Jericho is also an example of accepting the process before the purpose. The Israelites had just entered Canaan and began to conquer cities. In taking Jericho, God asked them to undergo a process of worship to get to the purpose. It was a picture of the process of winning spiritual battles through worship.

For six days they walked around the walls of Jericho blowing trumpets, then on the seventh day, they were to march seven times. On the seventh day when they marched seven times, they shouted out loud, as instructed as part of the process, and the walls came tumbling down. The city was theirs. The battle was won in the process of obedience and worship (Joshua 6:1-17).

Nothing happened for six days, not even during the first part of the seventh day. They had to trust God and be obedient. They had to trust God's process. They had to walk in obedience even when they did not understand.

This is how God works. He invites us into a divine process to bring His purposes into being. We can look at the coronavirus with anger and frustration, or we can rise to the occasion it presents. We can say we cannot understand this and give up, or we can go against our understanding and choose to trust Him. We can choose to rise to the occasion to trust Him and His process.

What is the Lord doing in us personally during this COVID-19 process? What is the church developing through this COVID-19 process? God is doing something. We cannot ignore this. He is working something important in the world and in us at this moment in history. Only when we allow the process to take its course will we benefit from the purposes God brings.

Rise to the Occasion *to Listen*

The world is very broken at the moment and the temptation is to not look at it. It's easier to ignore it. We would rather not show up when needed. As Christians we say a lot and do little about it. It's time to listen to the world's cry. It's time to get in tune with what the world needs. It's time to open our ears and hearts to really understand the world's pain during this pandemic.

What the world needs during this difficult time is for someone to listen. People around us want to be heard. They want to know they matter. One of the fruit of the Spirit is patience (Galatians 5:22), and it is a Christian virtue. Patience sits at the heart of listening.

Listening is uncomfortable. It requires much patience. It requires a desire to understand those we listen to. It requires sitting in discomfort over and over again. We need to listen, allowing people to finish speaking, allowing people to empty out what is on their minds. Only then can we really have a meaningful heart-to-heart talk. If we learn this simple lesson, we would get so much further in our ministry, in our commitment to sharing God's word.

Look at Jesus' interaction with the Samaritan woman at the well. He listened to her until she said it all, then He gave her the heart message that instantly turned her into an evangelist. This is how their conversation finishes, *"The woman said to him, 'I know that Messiah is coming (he who is called Christ). When he comes, he will tell us all things.' Jesus said to her, 'I who speak to you am he'"* (John 4:25-26).

After Jesus listened to her story, even her spiritual understanding, He could tell her, heart to heart, that He was Messiah. Jesus' listening skills and patience are amazing.

If we don't listen, we won't understand people, we won't understand what makes them tick, we won't understand what they love, we won't understand how valuable they are as people and what amazing contributions they can bring to God's kingdom.

Why would we expect people to listen to us if we don't listen to them first? How can we learn what they are going through without listening? When we listen to understand, we learn so much about them and so much about us. We learn how we need to position ourselves in order to have an impact on those we listen to.

Through empathetic listening we not only find out what people think and what they are afraid of, we also find out what they love. Love makes them sacrifice. Husbands sacrifice for their wives, parents for their children, and soldiers for their mates in the trenches. Our patience in listening should take us into a conversation about what people love; and when that happens, a real opportunity to talk about God's love is presented. There is no real conversation until extreme, intentional listening takes place first.

At the center of everything we do is love. Love is universal and people will feel it mostly when we patiently listen to them and take a real interest in their story. In that love they open up and become people of peace ready to receive the love of Christ you and I carry. Imagine if we practiced love and teach people to do the same.

Who still has this type of patience today? We love altar calls and mass evangelisms, yet we don't listen to the person next door to whom we wave daily. We forget the kingdom of God advances one person at a time. We forget every person matters and they are all God's creations waiting to identify with God as their Father. We cannot ignore our call to listen so we can show God's love.

Rise to the Occasion *to Lead*

Your family is watching you. Your church is watching you. Your neighbors are watching you. The world is watching you. If you are a pastor and a church leader, people are looking to you for leadership in this time. They want to see you lead yourself well and lead them responsibly.

Leaders lead. Leaders are at the top because they go first. They take every risk, first. That was the call of the apostle leader. They were first among the fivefold, not in a top down, but in a going first.

This is your call. Lead in this time. Take on the role to lead. You go toward danger, first. You do the uncomfortable, first. You listen, first. You love, first. You display faith, first. You give hope, first. You keep your mind sober, first. You talk to others, first.

When you do this, you will gain the most. The insights you receive from going first, the amount of value and the amount of connection you get from that, and the trust and the loyalty that you build in the process—all of that makes it worth your role as a leader.

Now is the time to be strong. Every test proves your strength not just your weakness. In this trial you have the opportunity to show how strong you are in your Christian conviction. Your conviction will ignite others' conviction. Your passion will inflame theirs. Your perseverance will propel theirs.

Lead in a way that makes people know they matter. Lead in a way that proves people are heard and seen, valued and dignified—that's what everyone wants, and you know that.

Give people the sense of belonging. There is no greater sense of love than belonging to the family of God. Our church people and those we witness to have this deep desire.

Give people a sense of purpose during this time. What do we offer our church people and also to the people outside the church? Are we inviting people to be part of our church family? Are we inviting them to belong to our ministry? Are we leading them into something worth going for? Are we inviting them to contribute? Does their contribution matter? Do they really matter?

In this season that divides and segregates, you can bring people together. You can help scared and lonely people belong to the family of God—a place with a purpose. Show them who you are and the Jesus who loves them.

As Christians we are so good at articulating what we are against, yet very rarely do we articulate what we are for. What is it that we are actually offering rather than, "Don't do this." Or, "Don't do that"?

As we lead during this time we should articulate better what we are for. Let's stop focusing on what we are against and highlight better and better what we are for. If we are to be the light of the world (Matthew 5:14), we should shine the light and darkness will flee. We are for God. We are for love. We are for service. We are for being salt and light. We have the solution in Christ for this and every crisis. We can do something about this situation. We have the truth. It's very simple.

We need to ask ourselves deeper and better questions to strengthen our leadership in this season.

What should we do in this time? What are the spiritual needs? What are the physical needs? What are the emotional needs? What are the connection needs? What precisely are we addressing? How are we answering those needs as a church in a real, pragmatic way? We must ask these questions and most importantly, after we answer each question, we must rise up to the occasion to lead.

Rise to *a Time Such as This*

The story of Esther is about a threat toward the Jews who are scattered throughout Persia after the Babylon exile. The king of Persia married Esther; and her cousin, Mordecai, who raised her because she was an orphan, challenges her to rise up to the occasion to save her people.

Then Mordecai told them to reply to Esther, "Do not think to yourself that in the king's palace you will escape any more than all the other Jews. For if you keep silent at this time, relief and deliverance will rise for the Jews from another place, but you and your father's house will perish. And who knows whether you have not come to the kingdom for such a time as this?" (Esther 4:13-14)

In a time of threat and danger for Esther and her nation, she has the opportunity to save herself and the Jews. But the risk is massive. She has to put her life on the line. And she did.

Esther understood her cousin's words. This was an opportunity she couldn't ignore. Even though everything was taken from her—her parents, her freedom, and her virginity—she arose to the occasion to save her people. God used her even though due to her gender, the culture, and the situation she seemed powerless and invisible. Yet God made her a formidable heroine, pivotal in Jewish history.

What if the current threats and uncertainties of the coronavirus give us an opportunity to stand up for God and His people? What if all we learned until now has prepared us for this? What if this is our finest period and the Lord challenges us to rise up in this time? What if this is our greatest hour as a church?

In a way we asked for this. We asked for a reset. We may have called it revival or awakening or something on those lines. If we search deep, we will find that we asked for an opportunity such as this for the church.

And now it is here. Now it's your time, it's our time. The world is united in isolation, fear, pain, grief, and uncertainty. The experience is common worldwide. The emotions are common. The world needs hope, light, direction. The people of the world need the children of God to rise up. They need you and me to rally the troops, the army of God to bring them hope and Him glory.

Let's not miss our hour, this time. 9/11 happened not so long ago. Did we take on the opportunity to do something amazing? What did we do afterward? We went back to work, back to shopping, back to our routine lives. We missed the *kairos* of that hour.

Let's not do that this time. We need to bring the story of the truth to light. Christianity needs a common language and a common story. This is new. It shouldn't be, but it is. We need to bring God's story into places where it is missing, where it is unpopular, and where we will be the minority.

We need to love with conviction like never before. We need to bring the heart of God into every sphere of society. There's too much ignorance, apathy, and unfortunate pockets of violence. There is no heart, conscience, and no moral responsibility in many regions of the world. We have become part of what we've allowed to happen. But now, the opportunity is here.

Something good can come out of the coronavirus, the lockdown, isolation, wearing masks, and of all the various restrictions we currently live with. Something good will come only if we choose, only if we are not naïve about what it is going to take. It takes courage, boldness, and conviction.

It's time to reflect. It's time to kneel, pray, meditate, and begin qualitative changes in our souls. It's time to put aside childish things now. We are not traumatized. This is not that difficult. Other generations were more traumatized than us. Get away from feeling victimized. Go up higher to soar above the storm. Walk on water.

Rise to the Occasion *to Walk on Water*

Take your chance as an individual and as a church to do something you may have never done before but always had on your heart.

Make yourself uncomfortable to make others better. Lose the fear. Tap into the courage.

People are open. The coronavirus has rocked everyone to the core; and in the process it cracked us all open. We needed this so we can go deeper. It's an extraordinary moment to be alive. We can be courageous now. Reform yourself and reform your church. Never before have you had this opportunity. Go for it!

Take time to conceive a new story that will begin in the very next moment as you finish reading this book. Give birth to the new story the Lord is depositing in you and has been depositing for a long time. Go deep to go high. And when you don't know where to go anymore, that's when your real life journey begins—when you get to the end of yourself, Jesus begins to shine.

Remember the story of Jesus, and then Peter, who walked on water? Let me recall it for you:

> *And in the fourth watch of the night he came to them, walking on the sea. But when the disciples saw him walking on the sea, they were terrified, and said, "It is a ghost!" and they cried out in fear. But immediately Jesus spoke to them, saying, "**Take heart; it is I. Do not be afraid.**" And Peter answered him, "Lord, if it is you, command me to come to you on the water." He said, "Come." So Peter got out of the boat and walked on the water and came to Jesus. But when he saw the wind, he was afraid, and beginning to sink he cried out, "Lord, save me." **Jesus immediately reached out his hand** and took hold of him, saying to him, "O you of little faith, why did you doubt?" And when they got into the boat, the wind ceased. And those in the boat worshiped him, saying, "Truly you are the Son of God"* (Matthew 14:25-33).

Jesus invites them to not be afraid as they see Him walking on water. Seeing Him perform the miracle was also an indirect invitation for them to be like Him and do what He does. But that initiative had to come from them.

We have our identity secured in Christ; and in this period, He is asking us not to be afraid but to step into that identity He has given us.

In essence, Peter was saying to the Lord, *"Lord, if it is You, just tell me and I will do what You are doing, I will come to You by walking on water."* Peter knows who Jesus is—the Messiah, the Christ. As he discovers who Jesus is, he finds his own identity in Him. If we are to get a true sense of our identity, we need to discover who Jesus truly is.

Whose idea was it to walk on water like Jesus? It was Peter's. He is the one who wants to walk like Jesus. It was his thought and his idea. He had childlike faith. If you show a child a trick, immediately he wants to do it too. Even though there is no trick here but faith, Peter who has immersed his identity into Christ's, is ready to practice his childlike faith. This is where we come in. All the dreams and ideas the Lord has put into our hearts can become realities if we allow and embrace a childlike faith.

Peter's idea was quite radical and a bit crazy. It's not usual to want to defy nature's laws. Walking on water is very unusual. But he brings it to Jesus and asks for a simple approval, essentially saying, "Lord, if You tell me to step out in my faith, in my identity, to become a water-walker and not just a talker, I am ready to do it." That's the initiative God wants from us during this time. To begin doing things that seem a bit ridiculous, where crazy faith is required.

Anyone thinking out loud would say to Peter, "You're crazy! You're out of your mind! You're losing it! Snap out of it! Jesus is God, you're not! Get over this silly idea!" Not Jesus, though. He was saying to Peter, "Come, walk in your faith! You can do it. But remember, you have to make the step. You step into your identity in Me. I am excited to see how much you can trust Me. Go on, test Me and test your faith."

Peter gets out of the boat and steps onto the water. And he walks. He walks in his faith and in his identity. His eyes are on Jesus and he walks on the water toward Jesus. Amazing story! This is not just Peter's story. This could be your story and my story.

But doubts will come into your mind. Even as you read this very passage you are already making up your mind about doubting and finding excuses not to rise to the occasion. Peter also became discouraged and almost sank. But Jesus grabs him instantly, challenging his doubt. It was an immediate response and rescue.

When we walk in our identity, when we rise to the call of God on our lives, when we walk on water, Jesus is with us—only an arm length away. And when the slightest doubt begins to sink us, He reaches out and grabs us. Peter's cry for salvation was not to his friends. It was to Jesus. He was closer. Peter was walking toward Jesus and in close proximity to Jesus. There was no one else closer. No one would be better positioned to save him than Jesus.

Peter stepped out of the boat—out of the normal, the comfortable, the predictable, the usual—into the unknown, into the new normal where faith had to be real. Peter's initial call was to be a fisher of men, not to walk on water. He could have remained comfortable in that call, yet he wanted more. No one else in the boat had the same desire for more, so no one else experienced what Peter did.

This is your call and your chance to step out of the old normal and into a new normal with Christ. This could be a new season where you walk on water, a new story where the narrative is supernatural, a new normal of life abundant.

As you do that, you will get a new song, a song not even the angels know, a song you can only learn here in the valley, in the process, and in the windy sea full of doubts. It is a song you learn when you trust Jesus to rise above the storm and walk on water.

And I heard a voice from heaven like the roar of many waters and like the sound of loud thunder. The voice I heard

*was like the sound of harpists playing on their harps, and
they were **singing a new song** before the throne and before
the four living creatures and before the elders. No one could
learn that song...* (Revelation 14:2-3).

The devil wants you to miss this opportunity. He wants you to be
side-tracked with the issues of the world. He wants you distracted.
He wants you emotionally trapped. He wants to steal this opportunity from you, to deny it. He wants you to be afraid of what the
media and the world portrays at the moment.

The vibe right now as I finish off the book in the middle of 2020
is that there may be a second wave of the pandemic. There are more
fears, more threats, and more doom days ahead according to the
media. And the devil laughs at how this hyperbole cripples us and
takes away the opportunities this season brings God's children. Let's
not be drawn into it but rise above it. Let's see the opportunity in
chaos. Let's move ahead into the new season.

Do not return to what was before. Do not return to the old
normal. Everyone talks about the new normal and no one knows
exactly what it will look like. There is a new normal in the church,
too. This excites me. Does it excite you or do you miss the good old
church days? Explore the new possibilities! Get out of the boat!

Recently the Lord reminded me that the depth of the water is
irrelevant when you walk on water. Also irrelevant is the depth of
the fear, the opposition, and all other challenges we may face. When
you walk on water, you are above it all. Your faith raises you above
all danger, no matter how big or wide. Take the step and walk in the
newness of the supernatural.

The new normal will be supernatural. The new normal will be
real. The new normal will see signs and wonders as the norm. The
new normal is Christ-centered. The new normal is kingdom priority. The new normal is discipleship engagement. The new normal is
life abundant.

If you are a pastor, this may have been what you had been preaching about and desiring for many years. It is the purpose you and your church have been preparing the new wineskin for. It is all you've been reading in this book and agreeing with. It is now here, at hand. Take it. Write your new story. Write your destiny. You have been prepared for this time. Everything you've learned and experienced until now has prepared you for this. Move into it and take your opportunity. Claim your inheritance. It is for you and your church. Let there be nothing lacking.

As a believer, what is holding you back from stepping into the new? What should you not go back to? Would you please write a list of what you will not return to? Would you take a few minutes and do this exercise for yourself and for your church? Will you be real? Will you go through the list and tick off each one as you ditch it? Will you unload the old normal to have the freedom to run into the new normal?

I leave you with the amazing perspective of the apostle Paul who took responsibility for his journey and made it his own. He made a conscious choice to press ahead by forgetting what was before, reaching forward by not looking back. And he invites us to have the same frame of thought and hold on to the truth attained so far:

> *Not that I have already obtained all this, or have already arrived at my goal, but **I press on** to take hold of that for which Christ Jesus took hold of me. Brothers and sisters, I do not consider myself yet to have taken hold of it. But one thing I do: **Forgetting what is behind and straining toward what is ahead, I press on toward the goal to win the prize for which God has called me heavenward in Christ Jesus.** All of us, then, who are mature should take such a view of things. And if on some point you think differently, that too God will make clear to you. Only let us live up to what we have already attained* (Philippians 3:12-16 NIV).

Paul's daily resilience is to press on, to strain forward, to struggle forward. This attitude kept him going to the end throughout all the challenges he faced in life. And if you and I want to be seasoned and mature in our walk with the Lord, we welcome this opportunity.

In a similar way, God invited His people in the past and us today to embrace the new season, the new normal—to perceive it, see it, and engage in it. It's an opportunity we cannot miss. Let's not go back to normal.

> *Remember not the former things, nor consider the things of old. Behold, I am doing a new thing; now it springs forth, do you not perceive it?* (Isaiah 43:18-19)

ONE APPLICATION

1. What one personal shift will you make from this book that will change your whole life from now on?

2. What one ministry shift will you apply from this book that will change the trajectory of your ministry from now on?

YOUR OPINION MATTERS TO US

Did *19 Covid Lessons the Church Cannot Ignore* impact you in some way?

Scan the QRCode below and let us know how this book helped you or your church grasp a different understanding of the Covid-related hardships.

or go to bit.ly/review_book_covid_church

Your honest feedback will help us improve our publishing ministry and allow more Christians worldwide to benefit from the wisdom you've read throughout these pages.

We will read each of your comments. Thank you in advance!

ABOUT THE AUTHOR

Dr. Natanael Costea (DMin, MA, BA) is an apostolic leader with a prophetic voice, a pastor, a strategist, a futurist, and an emotional intelligence coach. He is the founding director of Apostolic Churches Alliance and the principal of Australian School of Ministry. He is an ordained pastor and leads Menora Church in Perth, Australia.

His primary passion is for the gospel to be preached powerfully to all nations, making disciples of every nation. He engages in his passion in the marketplace by speaking and writing on emotional intelligence principles that lead to spiritual awakening and clarity.

After a seven-year career in the federal government of Australia and ten years leading a building development company, Dr. Costea established High EQ Australia, a not-for-profit training and coaching practice that supports his ministry.

He is the author of *Forty Years and Forty Days*, a practical discipleship book he wrote in forty days, starting on his fortieth birthday, and *The Most Precious Gift*, a book for those seeking a first encounter with God.

Dr. Costea, together with his wife, Raluca, and three young children, Evangeline, Isaac, and Menora, live in Churchlands, Western Australia.

Visit Natanael Costea Ministries at
www.natanaelcostea.com

Forty Years and Forty Days

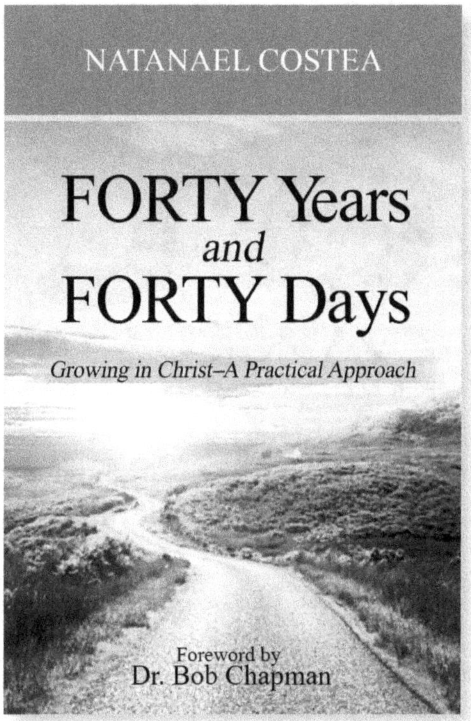

This practical and perfectly timed book comprises forty revelations in forty days during a period of prayer, fasting, and meditation—beginning on the author's fortieth birthday. His insights and personal experiences will enlighten and enliven your outlook on life, love, and liberty.

Published by
EVANGELISTA MEDIA & CONSULTING

publisher@evangelistamedia.com
www.evangelistamedia.com

 /evangelistamediaconsulting

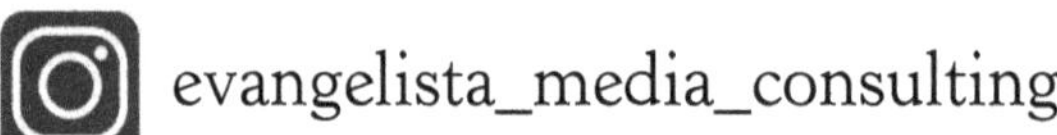 evangelista_media_consulting

www.ingramcontent.com/pod-product-compliance
Lightning Source LLC
LaVergne TN
LVHW020319200726
843507LV00012B/2161